THE
EXPERT
EXPERT

THE
EXPERT
EXPERT

THE PATH TO PROSPERITY AND PROMINENCE AS AN EXPERT WITNESS

DOUGLAS L. FIELD

iUniverse, Inc.
Bloomington

Legal Disclaimer and Warning
*This book is informational ONLY. Although the author is a licensed attorney, nothing contained in
it is offered in the manner of giving legal advice. The book is written with the understanding that and
purchasers specifically agree that the author is not rendering legal or other professional advice of any kind.
If the reader desires or requires legal advice, the services of a competent attorney should be sought. No
representation is made that this volume contains all information available on the subjects discussed. It
does not. The text offers general information only. The author is not engaged in giving legal advice on any
specific or general matter and shall have no legal liability or responsibility to any person or entity for loss or
damage caused or alleged to have been caused, whether directly or indirectly, as a result of any material or
information contained in the book. The law and statutes constantly change and it is not possible to predict
what developments may occur after publication of this volume. Every state and jurisdiction is distinct. Great
variability exists among expert professions and disciplines, among cases and situations in which experts are
employed, among attorneys who retain and use the services of experts and among experts themselves. In
the event of any doubt or if legal advice is required, please contact your attorney or retaining attorney.*

iUniverse books may be ordered through booksellers or by contacting:

*iUniverse
1663 Liberty Drive
Bloomington, IN 47403
www.iuniverse.com
1-800-Authors (1-800-288-4677)*

*Because of the dynamic nature of the Internet, any web addresses or links contained in
this book may have changed since publication and may no longer be valid. The views
expressed in this work are solely those of the author and do not necessarily reflect the views
of the publisher, and the publisher hereby disclaims any responsibility for them.*

*Any people depicted in stock imagery provided by Thinkstock are models,
and such images are being used for illustrative purposes only.*

Certain stock imagery © Thinkstock.

*ISBN: 978-1-4759-7171-2 (sc)
ISBN: 978-1-4759-7172-9 (hc)
ISBN: 978-1-4759-7173-6 (e)*

Library of Congress Control Number: 2013900790

Printed in the United States of America

iUniverse rev. date: 2/7/2013

To Sandy—
the wife of my youth, the wife of my life

And what does the LORD require of you

But to do justice ...

Micah 6:8

TABLE OF CONTENTS

PREFACE

I entered the practice of law in December 1973. After a very brief internship doing criminal work with a district attorney's office, I dedicated my career to civil trial practice. I worked in private firms for seven years and then had my own office for nearly eighteen years. This is called "panel counsel" in the trade. Then for fifteen more years, I worked for Farmers Insurance Exchange and its several affiliates as "staff counsel." In the later years, a management position at Farmers beckoned. I retired at the end of 2011 after several years as the managing attorney of Farmers' Branch Legal Office in Sacramento, California.

It was my privilege throughout all those years to work on a daily basis with expert witnesses from numerous and varying fields. Most frequently I dealt with physicians, osteopaths, podiatrists, dentists, and chiropractors of all specialties, but primarily orthopedic surgeons, neurologists, and neurosurgeons. For many years, I specialized in construction defect litigation. I worked closely with all manner of architects, engineers (civil, structural, and geotechnical), general contractors, and experts in several trades. These included grading and compaction, concrete, framing, plumbing, electrical, drywall, and roofing.

Also, of course, in conjunction with motor vehicle accident and premises liability cases, I met regularly with accident reconstructionists, biomechanical engineers, safety engineers, and tire and other product and premises defect experts. On many cases involving significantly large damages claims, I worked with accountants as well as utilization review, life care, and physical and occupational rehabilitation specialists. Finally, on not a few occasions I used the services of questioned documents and handwriting experts.

Exposure to these experts has run the gamut from basic consulting and solicitation of advice to full retention for all purposes, including examinations, event reconstructions, destructive testing, inspections, receipt of one or more reports, and preparation for and the giving of depositions and trial testimony. With great frequency, when I might not have retained one expert colleague or another, we would meet as opponents in cases. I would be the attorney taking their depositions in preparation for trial or cross-examining them on the witness stand in front of the jury.

Throughout the decades of my practice, the importance and prevalence of expert witnesses as key participants in the litigation process has grown. In the years when I emphasized management, I found that questions, issues, and conflicts involving experts (both those on our side and those opposing) were a weekly, if not even more frequent, concern. Much energy is devoted in the modern civil law firm to locating qualified experts, retaining their services, handling administrative matters with their offices, and preparing for and going to depositions and trial with them.

While I have, without qualification, liked, admired, and appreciated the learning and professionalism of many of the experts I have worked with, as with all human endeavors, the process has not been without its difficulties and challenges.

It seems to be the convention in the modern day for attorneys who retire to go into mediation and arbitration as a means of continuing to utilize their skill and learning to good effect. I considered this path but on reflection decided upon another way. I felt, based on much of what I had learned and observed over the years, that expert witness practice was an area where useful attention could be given and energy effectively devoted. The goal in mind would be significant general improvement of the practice of law and the overall administration of justice.

That, then, is the genesis of this book. In writing it, I have endeavored to comment meaningfully on the current state of the practice. I have sought to increase understanding and awareness among the non-legal professions of the law and the various constituencies that practice it. Included is some brief history of expert witness practice (we have not always had it!); the attempt is made to give a succinct background of the development of the law generally and of civil liability in particular. Even more especially, I have devoted chapters to liability insurance matters, as they figure greatly in the subject, and to the philosophy and practice of civil discovery, the arena in which most expert work occurs.

Much time is devoted to the subjects of depositions and trial testimony; to strategies, tactics, and techniques of direct and cross-examination; and to the question of expert and attorney preparedness. After that, there is discussion of various pitfalls and impediments and the rather quotidian matters of finance, money, and record keeping. Finally, I have taken the liberty to suggest establishing a formal certification for experts, to make a case for it, and to offer concrete suggestions as to what such a process might look like.

My topic is a large one, and it has proved to be an ambitious undertaking to cover it fully. However, recognizing that my potential readers are very, very busy with their practices and have limited time to devote to a volume such as this, I have decided to keep it to approximately two hundred pages. If, in keeping it to this moderate length, I have omitted to cover some detail or minutia, perhaps I will be forgiven.

I hope in putting this volume together that it might offer some small recompense to a profession that has served and treated me well for nearly forty years and that it might represent a help and a blessing to both lawyer and expert colleagues, known to me and unknown, as they continue their efforts in seeking and doing justice.

Douglas L. Field
Woodbridge, California
November 2012

ACKNOWLEDGMENTS

At the outset, permit me to remember several people who have assisted me greatly along the avenue of my legal career and in the production of this book. They include Marcia Rambo, formerly of Arroyo High School, San Lorenzo, California, and Charles R. Mack, Esq., formerly county counsel, Yolo County, California, both of whom were instrumental in teaching me how to write; the late Thomas McInerney, Esq., of Moraga, California, who more than anyone taught me to practice law; Russell W. Taylor, Esq., of Oakland, California, who was my loyal, dedicated, and tolerant law partner for nearly twenty years; Richard C. Valerian, Esq., of Oakland, California, who recruited me to Farmers and graciously supported my aspirations to get into management; Roger Favero and L. Stuart Girard, both of Exam Works, Rancho Cordova, California, who unstintingly supported and encouraged me in initiating and completing this effort; my daughter Julia C. Fikse, of Woodland Hills, California, herself a published author, who provided valuable practical advice; my son David M. Field, AIA, of Pleasant Hill, California, partner in a prominent Oakland, California architectural firm, who assisted me greatly in technical matters; and Sandra S. Field, my wife of nearly forty-four years who cheerfully put up with the book's entire long and involved writing process and who, when each draft was done, carefully and lovingly edited and corrected it. Without their friendship, mentorship, teaching, care, and affection, this book would never have been written.

INTRODUCTION:
FIRST THINGS FIRST

Out of my many excellent expert witness relationships over a long career in the law, one stands out as unique in the true sense of the word. It was genuinely one of a kind in effectiveness, efficiency, professional creativity, and just plain enjoyment. The expert was a physician, an emergency room specialist who had gone into consulting as a sideline to his ER practice. He was wholly steeped in medical knowledge and lore. He taught me how the practice of medicine is an art as well as a science. Off the top of his head, he could describe in detail even the most arcane conditions and syndromes. In addition, he had the quick and decisive mind of an emergency room doctor born of the need and habit of making urgent, life-and-death judgments, sometimes with less than optimal information. We worked dozens of cases together, and he frequently testified for me. His wife, his medical secretary, ran his office with unfailing precision. He never missed an appearance, and his reports were always timely and well written.

In those days, Zubin Mehta was music director of the Los Angeles Philharmonic Orchestra, and he frequently appeared with violinist Itzhak Perlman as featured soloist. If you watched them closely, you could see that Mehta and Perlman were both such thoroughgoing professionals, so comfortable with both their virtuosity and their art, that they often improvised in mid-concert, carrying out interpretations and subtleties to their music that gave it immensely added color and dimension.

In working with this ER physician we developed a similar level of professionalism, confidence and fluency. Even during live testimony, we could exchange a look that would suffice to settle on a new or different tactic or approach. Creativity and innovation were hallmarks of working with this expert. The level of trust and confidence that he engendered was remarkable, and he never failed to fully deliver as a professional consultant and expert witness. It will be the goal of this book to promote the creation of many more superb expert witness relationships like this one. It can be done, as this experience proved.

Where, then, to begin? It may be said that every law case has certain predictable elements. While they are not all always present, most customarily will be. The elements usually include interested parties, each with greater or lesser character, credibility, and potential jury appeal, and a factual pattern that will fall somewhere in the spectrum between intensely disputed all the way to essentially agreed upon. There also usually are percipient witnesses, each of variable reliability and veracity. Then come the expert witnesses, who are routinely individuals of great education and professional experience but are of widely varying learning and capability as witnesses. Finally, there will without fail be legal theories and strategies that are being executed by attorneys, also of significantly differing ability, dedication, and preparedness.

One of these usual elements is the subject matter of this book: experts and expert witness practice. The purpose is to set forth the current state of affairs in this critical facet of modern litigation and then to examine what may be done to improve it. Suggestions will be made as to specific and practical steps toward raising the level of practice in this field.

The effort will be worthwhile. Of all the standard elements of the typical litigation matter, it is expert witness practice (along with attorney practice) that is most readily susceptible to measurable improvement. The overall course of human affairs is of intense breadth and complexity. Efforts may be carried out with some marginal success, say, to reduce crime, or to promote safety, or to reduce product defects. Realistically, however, the normal and predictable activities of life will, in all probability, continue to generate conflict and contention. Similarly, the natural vicissitudes of personality and idiosyncrasy will forever render the prospect of improving the performance of both the interested parties and lay/percipient witnesses as elusive of predictability or consistency.

Limiting the hope for reform to the practice level of the professionals in litigation offers the greatest potential for measurable improvement. Here, improvement can be achieved by dint of analysis, study, teaching, and practical experience. Certainly the need for expert improvement crosses all boundaries among the medical, engineering, accounting, architectural, biomechanical, and accident reconstruction professions (just to list a few), on the one hand, and the legal profession on the other.

That this volume addresses the subject of practice by professionals other than attorneys by no means suggests that attorneys are immune from the need for improvement. They emphatically are not immune. However, raising the bar on attorney practice is left for another book.

Experts occupy a unique position in the litigation process. The law and the courts give them, by virtue of their education and experience, automatic authority and credibility. Since at its core a legal case is an in-depth examination of a series of past events, the legal process is unscientific, in that its subject matter is nonrepeatable. Even though law cases are not scientific in the classic sense, expert witnesses and their testimony are expected to inject a measure of scientific method and empirical certainty into the determination of cases.

In the modern era and in the popular view, science routinely holds high ground of credence, integrity, and certainty. In a car accident, it may be an obvious inference for the typical juror to draw from lay evidence, if, say, the vehicles were severely damaged, that one or both of them were traveling at excessive speed. However, expert accident reconstruction testimony (to cite only one example) mathematically and empirically quantifies the vehicle damage evidence. Thus it adds finite objectivity and academic cachet to the proof of an essential element of determining fault.

The great challenge for experts as they go through the court process is to preserve *to the end* the high level of credibility with which they start. While the legal system and jurors in particular are extremely generous in granting at the outset to experts the assumption of authority and truth, unhappily, this is all too easily and all too often quickly lost due to poor witness practices. Experts frequently (and unnecessarily) dissipate their initial standing in the eyes of the law. They do this through poor case preparation, poor forensic preparation, lack of teaching ability, and reliance upon faulty assumptions or contradictory statements. In addition, they often promote evidence of prejudice or bias, usually resulting from matters of money.

All of the foregoing can, with attention, study, and practice, be avoided.

The pages that follow will present in detail the information and skills necessary for the expert to preserve high standing to the end. Several considerations will be enumerated:

- Acquisition of a working knowledge of the law in terms of its history and development and also in terms of its day-to-day workings and processes.

- Development of familiarity with some legal principles, such as legal causation, that regularly operate in litigation matters.

- Awareness of the constituencies of the legal community, its various practitioners and their roles in operating the system, and development of habits and strategies for relating effectively with them.

- Promotion of a high-quality reputation in the legal community and opportunities for being regularly retained.

- Correct handling of communications, the development of records, and evidence and file management.

- Production, if and when required, of quality written reports that contain all essential elements, avoid common report writing pitfalls and form the firm foundation of the expert's participation in the case.

- Provision of consistently effective deposition testimony.

- Perfection of the ability to give persuasive, effective, and meaningful trial testimony.

- Handling of fees, payments, and other financial matters.

Investment of the time, effort, and treasure required to become a proficient expert witness will, by any measure, be well spent. Expert witness practice is undeniably lucrative. Fees are high. Overhead is low, especially in comparison with the maintenance of a full service professional office. Work is plentiful. Ours is an undeniably litigious society. All talk of lawsuit reform aside, Americans continue to sue each other with gusto, and no slackening of the current pace appears to be on the horizon.

In the medical field, for example, expert witness practice has additional appeal in view of the ever-greater intrusion of government and government regulation into the practice of medicine. Bureaucratic rules, regulations, and fee restrictions do not (as of yet, anyway) apply in this area of activity, and the practitioner may charge and collect the full measure that the market allows.

Significant dedication and diligence is required to make and to keep one's reputation as a capable and credible expert witness. But it is effort that in the end well remunerates the one who makes it. Even more, the elevation of expert practice has collateral benefits of great importance to society as a whole. Not the least of these is the promotion, as we will see, of a commensurate elevation in the quality of legal practice and, most enduringly of all, the promise of raising the frequency that real and true justice is achieved in the courts.

In summary, it is the intention of this volume first to explore the history and details of the legal framework in which expert witness practice operates and that make it so significant in modern law. This will include the vital element of the law that relates to insurance policies and the parties to them. It will include a brief discussion of how insurance claims are handled.

Next, its purpose is to recognize various weaknesses and shortcomings attributable to those participants who are diminishing overall effectiveness.

The heart of the book will be a detailed discussion and study of ways and means to significantly improve expert witness practice, particularly as it relates to report writing and testifying at deposition and at trial. Housekeeping matters of record keeping, billing, securing business, and common pitfalls will be discussed in detail.

Finally, a case will be offered for the establishment of a process for conferring formal designation on experts that attests to their qualifications, learning, and preparedness as well as their competency and effectiveness *as witnesses*.

The power of meaningful illustration will be one of the theses of this book. In keeping with that, it has been salted with anecdotal examples, stories, and events that provide good examples of the points being made. To paraphrase Jack Webb's introductory riff on the old *Dragnet* television program, "the stories you are about to read are true; the names have been omitted or changed to protect the innocent." (And in many cases here, the guilty as well!)

What, then, is the current state of expert witness practice? How does the state of expert preparedness in the realm of their strictly professional expertise relate to their preparedness and their ability as expert witnesses? How capable are they as report writers and as witnesses in deposition and at trial? The following chapter addresses these questions and suggests a starting point for increasing proficiency.

CHAPTER ONE

TURNING EXPERTS INTO EXPERT WITNESSES
PRELIMINARY PRINCIPLES

Any thoughtful reflection on the challenges of managing a large civil trial practice soon settles on the question of expert witnesses. Experience indicates that in a typically busy practice, expert witness problems arise at least weekly. Expert issues, what is more, are almost never routine or simple administrative matters that can be easily dealt with. They are almost always of crucial importance to the individual case in which they arise. By extension, then, they have ramifications that affect the entire law office. Whether as catastrophic as an expert's complete disintegration/collapse on the witness stand at trial or as simple as fractiousness in scheduling and calendaring, these failures cannot be ignored. They require the commitment of significant resources of time and energy for resolution. And frequently their impact is significantly negative on case outcome.

Expert witness problems can be grouped into three general areas.

First, difficulties often are generated by a lack of contextual understanding on the part of the expert of the peculiarities of the legal system and the courts. Much confusion results from the reality that assumptions and practices taken for granted by lawyers and judges are quite distinct from those that operate in other professional disciplines.

Next, there are breakdowns in good communication. These breakdowns result from failure to ensure explicit understanding between the referring attorney and the expert as to the purpose and scope of the assignment, the preparation of formal reports, and the provision of quality deposition/trial testimony. Regardless of the source, communications confusion is repeatedly experienced in expert witness practice.

Finally, lack of collaboration in administrative matters of arranging examinations, inspections, meetings, depositions, and court appearances are a continual frustration.

It is occasionally (and mistakenly) said, "Leaders are born, not made." By extension it is also commonly, and again incorrectly, thought that a good expert witness is either naturally born to the work or not, and that skill as a witness cannot be taught. It is the thesis of this chapter that with reasonable and effective teaching, anyone with the native ability and faculties to attain the status of expert can, in addition, learn to be a good expert witness.

Specific and intentional education to achieve the foregoing is needful. It should comprise a carefully crafted curriculum of study with interactive elements that document progress and recognize and certify successful completion. Attention to the three concepts of *context, communication*, and *cooperation* forms a workable framework for appreciating how the witness potential and capability of experts can be markedly improved and is a point of departure for developing teaching strategies and curricula.

I. Context

The context of expert witness activity is the modern legal system and the courts. Therefore, a rudimentary understanding on the part of the expert of how and why the law and the courts function as they do is essential. Most experts are learned in some scientific field of inquiry. Medicine, engineering of all kinds, architecture, biomechanics, accident reconstruction, and accounting (to list only a few obvious examples) are all firmly rooted in scientific inquiry and the scientific method. All these disciplines rely fundamentally on observability, repeatability, and verifiability as the bases for the inquiry that undergirds their conclusions.

Law is unscientific in the sense that at its core, a legal case involves the process of reconstructing a single, unique past event, a past event that by nature is no longer observable or repeatable. Law is much less rooted in scientific method than it is in historical method and in promoting a fair and accurate reconstruction of the event upon which legal conclusions can be drawn and decisions made. Experts should understand that the epistemology of the law (that is, the way the law learns what it learns and knows what it knows) is altogether different from that of their own disciplines. In practical fact, this means that the expert's interaction will not usually be with other persons of scientific training and assumptions, but persons trained in history, rhetoric, English, and political science. One might profitably think of them as people who prefer crossword puzzles to Sudoku. Much confusion is generated between attorneys and their experts as a result of this underlying and dramatic difference in basic assumptions.

Inasmuch as expert witnesses undertake to expand their practices into the legal arena, they should anticipate and be prepared for the fact that referring attorneys expect them to be willing to commit to acquiring a working knowledge of the legal system and the hows and whys of its operation. Any effort directed toward preparing experts for effective witness work must consider as of first importance the context of the legal system, its historical development, and its current manner of operation.

II. Communication

Having cleared away the confusions created by poor contextual understanding, the improvement of all aspects of communication between experts and their referring attorneys is the next order of business. Capable expert witnesses need to be able to effectively impart information as well as also to demand it. Good expert communication starts with an expert who is able to demand from the referring attorney all of the information and details necessary both to understand the purpose and scope of referral and to complete the assignment. Any expert should feel free, not only at the time of referral but also throughout the pendency of the assignment, to contact the referring attorney and secure all necessary information and assistance.

Having thoroughly and completely understood the assignment and completed it with the utmost of professional ability and zeal, experts next face the challenge of communicating their opinions and conclusions in three different realms: (1) the report, (2) the deposition, and (3) testimony at trial. Obviously not all referrals involve every type of communication. Most assignments (in particular medical ones) will require a report. Some entail giving a deposition. Very few, but a significant number nevertheless, will require an appearance at trial.

Each of these communication events is distinct and requires the development of different skills. However, the order in which they occur is important, and each event builds upon the other. The preparation of a high-quality report forms the basis for effective deposition testimony. Then the giving of a good deposition, if it does not avoid the need for trial altogether, is essential in being prepared for a good jury presentation.

The specifics of the subject of communication are diverse and complicated, but it cannot be overemphasized that the development of superior expert witness communication skills is the axis upon which the entire effort turns. Their development alone will promote the other two elements of context and cooperation. Teaching good, full-spectrum communication by way of report writing, deposition testimony, and trial presentation is the essence of improving expert witness effectiveness.

III. Cooperation

After securing good contextual understanding and excellent communication, brief attention to the matter of mutual cooperation is warranted. Legal people often experience many challenges when attempting to secure examination and deposition dates from experts. Horrifyingly worse, from the perspective of the referring attorney, is being told that that the medical expert, as only one example, is unable to attend trial as scheduled due to an emergency surgery. It might be thought, particularly in view of the significant money that is invested in experts, that a high level of cooperation in scheduling and appearing for depositions and trial would go without saying. Recent experience demonstrates that it often does not.

No expert should undertake legal work without first fully understanding the practical requirements that it will entail. Trials are set months, even as much as a year, in advance of their start dates. In most states and in the federal courts, there is a detailed pretrial expert disclosure procedure that has numerous date-sensitive and inviolable time deadlines. Experts will be required to respond fully to the quotidian exigencies of legal work in terms of being willing to appear on comparatively short notice and to be patient with the numerous continuances and postponements, which always seem to characterize the legal process and which usually result from actions and considerations entirely beyond the control of the referring attorney.

Mutual cooperation is best secured through education. When the parties to expert witness practice clearly understand each other's demands, pressures, and professional obligations, the road to success is made easier. Although basic, some might say obvious, careful attention to full professional cooperation will be required in any process designed to develop better expert witnesses.

It is hoped this analysis demonstrates the reality that while expert witness practice is fraught with pitfalls for all concerned, they are not insurmountable. A comprehensive and carefully thought out training effort to teach experts to become good witnesses can readily be developed and will achieve commendable results. These results will measurably raise the quality of expert witness practice and testimony and will have the notable collateral benefit of lifting the quality of practice of all professionals involved and promote the effective administration of justice generally.

Experts are routinely learned and well qualified in their fields of study, certification, and experience. This does not necessarily mean, however, that they are automatically schooled and competent in performing as efficient participants in the legal process and as effective witnesses. While this next level of preparation is intricate and involved, good educational processes, curricula, and practical experience will adequately address any deficiencies.

This process of securing significant overall improvement of expert witness practice starts with a good working knowledge of the various constituencies who practice law and operate the courts. After that, there is needed a healthy appreciation of the challenges that confront experts on a daily basis. Finally, a brief discussion of experts and their offices, on the one hand, and legal people, on the other, will help each to understand how both can most effectively work together.

CHAPTER TWO

THE CARE AND FEEDING OF LEGAL PEOPLE: HOW TO WORK TOGETHER EFFECTIVELY

The courts, litigation attorneys, and their offices deal with experts, their offices and administrative personnel, and expert issues every day. From the perspective of legal people, these encounters are routinely frustrating, difficult, and many times unrewarding. This is by no means to fix blame on nonlegal professionals, but it does point out the need for much greater mutual understanding of common and competing professional wants and needs. What follows represents the viewpoint from the legal side as to how expert professionals can better understand and address the exigencies of legal practice at those frequent times when the respective practices coincide (not to say collide!).

It should be recognized as a first order of business that a certain unavoidable symbiosis exists among the professions, such that awareness and embracing of the need to work together will promote more effective collaboration for the greater good of all. Further, legal practitioners fall into several categories, whose challenges and work routines are quite distinct from one another. They require separate understanding by those on the expert practitioner side. Finally, a number of practical suggestions for easing our joint path can be readily identified.

(It is candidly acknowledged that these observations are produced from the vantage point of a legal professional looking at other professions.

It is to be hoped that a similar commentary might be forthcoming from the nonlegal perspective looking at the legal side. It would be gratefully received and carefully considered.)

The Reluctant Symbiosis

Howsoever unenthusiastically it may often be embraced, the symbiotic relationship between the nonlegal, especially medical, professions and the legal profession is inevitable and indissoluble. Medical issues, as a notable example, are central to (in some cases absolutely essential to) a significant number of prevalent areas of the law. These include personal injury law, family law, criminal law, and workers' compensation. Public entity law, corporate law, contract law, or real estate law are not thusly grounded. The legal areas listed above where medicine, again by way of example, and law cross intimately affect the lives, freedoms, and livelihoods of the litigants much more than in other areas.

The professional code of ethics for the medical profession obliges physicians as citizens to assist in the administration of justice.[1]

The significance to society of our professions closely interacting is difficult to overstate.

The relationship between medicine and the law stands as an excellent starting point for illustration of the close relationship that at all times and in all circumstances exists between the various professions and the law. The following discussion emphasizes medicine but may be applied to other professions.

The proportion of legal cases in which the medical or psychological health of litigants, parties, or witnesses has been placed in issue is extraordinarily high, and the result is that all medical personnel who have treated these persons are likely to become involved in their legal cases.

---

1   American Medical Association, Code of Medical Ethics, Opinion 9.07, Statements of the American College of Surgeons, ST-8, American Academy of Orthopedic Surgeons, Code of Ethics for Orthopedic Surgeons, Section V.C.

Medical issues represent essential inquiries in most injury cases, at both the claims and litigation stages. Lawyers, judges, and juries are dependent on the medical profession to explain, objectify, and predict the future of a litigant's medical situation.

Our societal vehicles for the compensation of injuries and the determination of criminal guilt or innocence cannot operate without medical participation.

Conversely, medicine depends on the legal profession for the social and financial stability needed for it to flourish. In no small measure, the law is a benefits delivery system that provides the equitable, orderly, and enforceable delivery of monetary assets to those who require medical care. When it works as intended, recipients of benefits will in turn compensate the people who are caring for them (and who often will need to continue to care for them on into the future). Courts, judges, and attorneys operate the system that secures the stream of commerce that enables effective medical practice to occur in peace, stability, security, and prosperity.

It is not possible to practice medicine in a vacuum where the law does not intrude.

There is, thus, an unavoidable interdependence between the medical and legal professions that their practitioners are left without alternative but to warmly accept and willingly embrace. Practitioners of other professions will appreciate that similar symbiosis exists between their professions and the legal profession and will likewise recognize the importance of mutual cooperation and understanding.

Full appreciation of the legal side of this equation starts with description of the various practitioners of our profession and the ways in which their activities fit into the whole of the practice of law.

Dramatis Personae:
The Legal Cast of Characters

The principal groups of legal people that expert professionals can expect to encounter are judges, juries, attorneys, paralegals, and legal secretaries. Each group has its distinct professional and administrative challenges, and effective collaboration will recognize these and respond to them.

Judges: Judges have the fundamental role of acting as referees of the legal process and of ensuring fairness, promptness, and efficiency. In most jurisdictions they are, in one way or another, elected, so there is a political component to their practice and outlook. Significant authority is reposed in judges. They are, without a doubt, legally and ethically obligated to follow the law. They do, however, have wide discretion. Incorrect rulings are subject to appeal, but in the case of exercise of discretion, their decisions are appealable only upon abuse of discretion—a standard rarely proved.

Like all people, judges have their individual political and sociological ethos that often figures into their rulings and into the exercise of their discretion. Judges occupy a position of high prestige, and their positions, for the obvious reasons of promoting stability and consistency, are very secure. They thus can be autocratic and inflexible. Many are very creative thinkers and proud of it. They can be unpredictable, and their rulings, even in jury matters, can eviscerate an attorney's case very suddenly and unexpectedly.

From the standpoint of experts and their administrative assistants, it is critical to bear in mind that one of the tasks that judges take very seriously (and, ironically, with wide variance in effectiveness) is the need to move matters along quickly and expeditiously—especially during a jury trial. A judge's most common exposure to the voting public is to jurors, both in the pretrial selection pool and after empanelment. Judges are very sensitive to the hardship and disruption that jury service occasions to the average citizen, and they are at pains to communicate in word and deed their commitment to minimizing that disruption.

Everyone involved in legal work, including expert practitioners, needs to be prepared to comply with the judge's scheduling requirements. Trials are calendared months in advance. The parties are expected to be ready at all stages to proceed quickly, efficiently, and without interruption. Attorneys are expected to have a steady flow of witnesses present at court and to be ready to proceed without delay. There is little tolerance for wasting the time of twelve people randomly drawn from the community waiting on the arrival, say, of a doctor who is delayed completing rounds, seeing patients, or in surgery. All experts who elect to become involved in legal work must be prepared to do what judges want when they want it.

In recent years, most states have enacted legislation designed to promote speedier civil litigation. These acts to reduce trial court delays are sometimes called "fast-track rules" or "the rocket docket." The obligation for promoting compliance falls upon the judges, and they and the court administrative personnel who support them are intensely serious about ensuring their success. Little or no flexibility can be expected from the judges or clerks in moving cases forward in compliance with these rules.

Juries: While not strictly "legal people," jurors come into the legal arena under compulsion of law and under the direct control and supervision of judges. Juror pools (by design) represent the mainstream of the communities from which they are drawn. Individually and outside the context of jury duty, jurors ideally are average citizens who generally fit the profile of most typical medical and chiropractic patients, users of accounting services, and legal clients. However, whereas on the outside they come as patients and clients with a high level of trust and deference, they take their civic duty as jurors very seriously and tend, on the inside as jurors, to be somewhat cynical, holding all professionals to the highest standards of objectivity, integrity, and professionalism.

Jurors as jurors do not automatically trust professionals, as they do when they go to them for professional services. (Interestingly enough, they usually trust the judge implicitly.) The credibility that professionals have with these people as patients and clients is not present when they encounter the very same people as jurors. At court, interaction with them must recognize their independent spirit and dedication to duty.

Attorneys: In the expert witness field, attorneys are the customers. They make the decisions that an expert's services are needed and decide whom to use. These decisions may be made in consultation with clients and insurance claims representatives as appropriate, but attorneys are responsible for and direct the strategy of litigation, and ultimately the choice of an expert practitioner rests with them.

Most attorneys are extraordinarily busy. Civil defense attorneys manage caseloads of fifty to seventy (and occasionally even more) cases (depending on complexity) at any one time. Cases last, with some notable exceptions, from eighteen to thirty months. Civil defense attorneys try to resolve sixty-five to seventy-five cases per year, whether by settlement or by trial. Roughly 97 percent of all civil cases are settled without trial.

All cases, however, are worked up as if they will go to trial. There is no rule of thumb as to which cases will go to trial and which will settle. Cases representing the full spectrum of complexity and size are regularly tried. Virtually no case is too small or too big to be tried. The 3 percent of cases that go to trial receive even more intense preparation and scrutiny.

It is essential that at least some cases be tried, as trial is the only benchmark by which the value of cases generally can be determined and updated. It is not anticipated that the ratio of cases tried to those that are settled will change in the foreseeable future.

The life of a civil case goes through several generally predictable stages including the prelitigation, pleading, discovery, expert, mediation/arbitration, and, if necessary, trial stages. There are routine activities which attorneys must initiate and complete in each stage including depositions, obtaining of medical and employment records, preparation for and participation in mediation and settlement conferences, initiating and responding to written discovery requests, court-ordered arbitration, and extensive pretrial and actual trial activities.

Since the involvement of many other unpredictable players is always a factor at all stages, attorneys often have less control over both the timing and outcomes of events that they participate in than do their nonlegal expert counterparts. Attorneys expend extensive effort in determining and initiating the correct activities on their cases, and then they are constrained to deal with the results, however they fall. Attorneys and their cases are continually vulnerable to the capriciousness of judges, client and witness breakdowns, the vicissitudes of claims handling protocols, and dissatisfaction and second-guessing by various stakeholders.

Considering the press of business that attorneys are under and the uncertainties of law practice generally, expert witnesses colleagues can constructively facilitate the process by insisting that attorneys be very clear as to what it is that they are asking for.

Often attorneys who have not recently had the time for and luxury of carefully reviewing and updating current case strategy and tactics contact experts to make referrals. Demanding strict clarity of the expert's assignment as apart of the referral process will assist (dare we say compel?) attorneys in reviewing and rethinking their cases through in light of current developments to the mutual benefit of both professionals.

It is to be borne in mind also that attorneys are "word people." Most are almost exclusively trained in liberal arts disciplines, such as English, rhetoric, history, political science, sociology, and philosophy. Few are scientists or are familiar with scientific method, mathematics, or statistics. Attorneys, on the other hand, are good wordsmiths. They know how to write and how to speak.

My firm occasionally retained a noted and respected surgeon for consultation and independent medical examinations. He was preeminently qualified in his specialty and was the premier surgeon in his geographical area for the most delicate and complex surgical matters that arose in his specialty. He was especially famous for treating severely injured accident victims. He had a comparatively conservative outlook overall and so was popular with civil defendants' attorneys.

The difficulty in using him was that his reports were the essence of perfunctory. They were routinely sprinkled with medical shorthand and jargon that was difficult for nonphysicians to understand. He wrote in phrases and regularly eschewed the complete sentence. His letters were cast in the manner of stream of conscious narrative and lacked commonly accepted elements of organization. He never came to appreciate that his written reports were the face he presented to the community. They were in utter contrast to his otherwise superb qualifications, but they were, unless he happened to give his deposition, all that was ever seen of him. His poor writing needlessly detracted from his overall presentation.

This expert's inability to conform to the basic requirements of good written communication demonstrates how formal reports and communications need to be properly written. The use of good grammar and complete sentences is non-negotiable. Decades of reading expert reports and cross-examining experts on their reports in deposition and at trial has demonstrated, as is commented upon at length in chapter 9, that the inartful selection of vocabulary, phrases and figures of speech often measurably diminishes the impact and clarity of report writing. Terms of professional significance should be defined. Reports must be well organized, concise, cogent, and complete. Experts must have a thorough and complete understanding of critical concepts, including especially causation, from the legal perspective.

The daily exigencies and practicalities of the practice of law in terms of calendaring, dates, appointments, and time management are much more fluid than in other types of practice. Patience is required with attorneys' need for great flexibility in changing appointments, deposition dates, and trial dates. Circumstances that are beyond their control usually impose calendaring changes on attorneys rather than vice versa. Rushes are unavoidable in the practice of law, particularly in view of civil trial delay reduction statutes. Attorneys need their colleagues in other professions to understand and be willing participants in dealing with frequent scheduling changes.

As a result of the time constraints that attorneys are under, they tend to have "go-to" doctors and other experts. These experts are those whose professionalism is unparalleled; who are good writers, testifiers, and overall communicators; who understand the interrelationship between their own professions and the law; and who cooperate in and facilitate the administrative aspects of our joint professional practices.

Paralegals: This is something of a hybrid position, in that paralegals have significant legal training but are not permitted to represent clients. Their work is not clerical, per se, but it is administrative and occasionally overlaps secretarial duties. Typically paralegals receive medical and other records and put them in useful order for their attorneys. They may review and summarize medical or other records, plans, and documents. They propound and respond to written discovery. In this connection, they have extensive client and witness contact. They become intimately familiar with each file.

The entire concept of a paralegal is that they have the time and resources to patiently and thoroughly study and understand case files. As such, paralegals frequently live in a sort of "quiet backwater" in the law office, and they can be an excellent resource to experts, in that they are usually very conversant with all case particulars and can provide complete and up-to-date information on case requirements.

Legal Secretaries: These people are greatly influential in all matters of interface between legal and other practices. They are massively busy on a daily basis with coordination and scheduling/rescheduling of multitudinous appearances, depositions, independent medical examinations, arbitrations, mediation hearings, and trials. Court clerks and opposing attorneys, paralegals, and secretaries regularly subject legal secretaries to vitriol, verbal abuse, and all forms of unkindness.

Typically the legal secretary will receive and be tasked with effectuating the request for site and vehicle inspections as well as independent medical examinations with the expert whom the attorney has chosen. It is the attorney who will specify the expert with whom the inspection or examination is to be set. However, when the secretary begins the process, the attorney will often be out of the office on other business. If there are impediments with the attorney's first choice of expert, the secretary may have discretion to move to another individual and, in any event, certainly will have influence on that choice. The legal secretary's criteria in preferring one practitioner over another will be in matters of ease of scheduling, congeniality of office personnel, and overall administrative efficiency. Keeping the legal secretary happy is a matter of first importance to the medical-legal practitioner.

Nothing Consists Like Consistency

If there is a single virtue that marks out the successful and desired expert professional, it is consistency. From the standpoint of all of the groups of legal people detailed above, the physician, psychologist, chiropractor, architect, general contractor, engineer, or accident reconstructionist (and their office personnel) who is most consistent will most frequently be retained.

Consistency starts with a thorough, objective, and complete investigation, examination, and records review. This is then documented by a clear, concise, and readable report that addresses all activities undertaken in furtherance of the assignment along with the examiner's opinions, reflecting a correct understanding of applicable legal principles that are raised. Thus is laid the foundation for a clear and effective deposition in advance of trial and then for equally effective trial testimony.

Attorneys and courts handle relatively fewer matters, and each matter takes relatively longer than nonlegal matters. Thus, it is fair to appreciate that legal matters are considered in intense and exhaustive detail for periods of time and then are set aside in favor of other matters until some weeks, months, or even years later, when they are brought back for additional close scrutiny. Consistency among the investigation, examination, report, deposition, and trial testimony is the best prescription for addressing these time lapses and for not losing connection, cohesion, and coherence as a result of them.

Carrying forward consistently from a high-quality exam and report through deposition and trial testimony promotes confidence both in the expert witness and in the legal practitioner at each stage of the legal process. Worries over the lines of attack that opposing counsel may take are reduced or eliminated altogether through consistency. Then as the expert practitioner builds the professional expert practice and completes greater and greater numbers of investigations, examinations, depositions, and trial appearances, this consistency constructs a strong fortress of credibility and trust that is immensely difficult to undermine.

Consistency is demonstrated as well in the more mundane matters of scheduling, timeliness, office efficiency, and "user friendliness." All who undertake expert legal work need to be acutely aware of the day-to-day challenges that face legal people in dealing with the courts, arbitrators, mediators, and other law offices. They must participate in the processes by quickly and efficiently collaborating in all scheduling and deadline matters and by being utterly faithful in making all inspection, examination, deposition, and trial commitments.

Little is more discouraging or frustrating to an attorney and staff than to hear at the end of two years of painstaking preparation that the retained expert cannot attend the long-set and anxiously anticipated trial due to other professional commitments or a prepaid vacation. On the other hand, that expert who can consistently be relied upon to cooperate in housekeeping matters, meet deadlines, and appear when and where required will always be highly prized.

Easy Does It

Making it easy to work with the expert's office is the overarching principle of successful relations with legal people. It has been said that selection of medical experts can be likened to a favorite baseball glove. One may have available a brand new glove with all the latest advancements and features, but the one most likely to be picked up and used is the old one that is the favorite, the one that the lawyer is used to and that has always performed reliably.

This represents a good illustration that whether the expert professional is a regular choice or is receiving a first-time referral, all that is done to make it easy for the lawyer to use that expert, and all that is done to ensure consistency, reliability, and efficiency, secures the expert professional's status as the comfortable, favorite, preferred professional.

In undertaking expert witness practice, all professionals should commit at the outset to be easy to work with. Acting as an expert witness is a service business, and once an assignment is taken on, the attorney is a customer, as much as are the expert's regular patients or clients. Attorneys are prepared willingly to invest heavily in expert participation in their cases, and in return, they need and deserve the expert's best consistent, energetic, and cheerful effort.

Although starkly different in almost every way, the various professions are inextricably linked, and society depends upon and requires them to work effectively and efficiently together. When they do, society as a whole is greatly benefited and justice is served.

Having considered in detail the relationship between the legal profession and those professions that regularly provide experts who participate in law cases, and having rehearsed the several groups of legal professionals who operate the court system, it is now appropriate to narrow our inquiry to the legal activities and principles that the professional will participate in. As a matter of first instance, we consider the question of exactly what an expert witness is and how the use of expert witnesses has developed in the continually evolving practice of law.

CHAPTER THREE

WHAT IS AN EXPERT WITNESS?

Expert witnesses occupy a unique position in the legal system, conferred upon no other class of witness. Expert witnesses are also occasionally referred to as "professional witnesses" or "judicial witnesses." They are individuals whose education, skill, experience, training, and specialized knowledge exceed that of the layperson. They, thus, are accorded and permitted the following:

- to have the court or jury officially and legally *rely on their professional, scientific, or technical opinion* about a factual or evidentiary issue within the scope of the expert's field of specialty by way of assistance to the fact finder[2] (either the jury or the judge or an arbitrator considering the case without a jury)

- to respond to hypothetical questions[3]

- to rely on data and facts used by others in the field, even if the evidence relied upon would otherwise be hearsay or otherwise inadmissible[4]

- to provide evidence about facts within their field of expertise[5]

---

2   See, e.g., Federal Rule of Evidence 702 as amended 2000 and 2011.

3   California Civil Instructions (CACI), No. 220, *Experts: Questions Containing Assumed Facts.*

4   CACI, No. 219, *Expert Witness Testimony.*

5   Ibid.

The latitude and privilege granted to experts is remarkable. They are, by virtue of their learning and experience, permitted to testify as to their opinions despite the fact that they may not have actually witnessed the events involved in the trial. Experts take the stand already clothed in the mantle of assumed believability and reliability as witnesses.

Nonexpert (or percipient) witnesses are required to confine their testimony to events or matters of which they have personal knowledge; that is to say, what they have personally perceived. The availability to experts of their opinions as evidence expands exponentially the scope of their potential testimony. It opens broad areas for the introduction of personal belief and conviction, resulting in opportunity for the exercise of persuasive power and didactic giftedness.

Similarly, the practice that experts are allowed to respond to hypothetical questions additionally opens wide panoramas of inquiry that could never be reached through the evidence of percipient witnesses alone. With the limitation that the assumed facts in a hypothetical question must be true, the availability to them of the hypothetical question expands immensely the possible reach of expert testimony. Also, however, when used in the hands of a skillful cross-examining attorney, hypothetical questions open up the possibility for many pitfalls and the potential to discredit the expert witness.

No other class of witness is permitted to rely upon the out-of-court statements and writings of persons not present before the court. The expert may be (and frequently is) used to bring evidence before the court and jury which otherwise might not be available.

Experts may acquire and amass data. They act as arbiters and tutors of the principles and practices of their professions and are repositories for the learning contained in their professional areas. They are a resource for the summarization and synthesis of that learning.

Experts are regularly used for the offering of their opinions on an incredibly broad range of subjects, in both the criminal and civil arenas. The specific facts of incidents, accidents, and events are regularly the subject of expert evidence including accident reconstruction; biomechanical engineering; civil, structural, and geotechnical engineering; forensic accounting; and economics.

In personal injury matters, medical experts testify literally every day as to severity of injury, medical expenses (both past and future), loss of earnings and earning capacity, extent of disability, as well as impairment and disfigurement.

Experts assess intellectual property and medical negligence cases. They are called upon to assess damages and costs in construction defects matters, both simple and complex. Experts in both criminal and civil cases regularly address fingerprinting, DNA and blood analysis, and issues of mental health and insanity. Proof of defects in machinery and other types of products is steeped in expert evidence.

Nevertheless, the scope of allowable expert opinion making is not unlimited. In the early part of the twentieth century, the general rule of admissibility of expert testimony regarding novel scientific propositions was whether it had "gained general acceptance in the particular field in which it belongs."[6] Starting in 1993, however, a series of cases before the Supreme Court of the United States, sometimes called the Daubert Trilogy,[7] articulated a new, narrower, and more refined standard.

This series of cases confirmed the role of the trial judge as gatekeeper in assuring that scientific expert testimony truly proceeds from scientific knowledge. In addition, the trial judge is tasked with ensuring that the expert's testimony is "relevant to the task at hand." The judge must find that it is more likely than not that the expert's methods are reliable and reliably applied to the facts at hand.[8]

---

6   Frye v. United States, 293 F. 1013 (D.C. Cir. 1923).

7   Daubert v. Merrill Dow Pharmaceuticals, Inc., 509 U.S. 579, 113, S. Ct. 2786, 125 L.; Ed. 469 (1993); General Electric Co. v. Joiner, 522 U.S. 136, 118 S. Ct. 512, 139 L. Ed. 2d 508 (1997); Kumho Tire Co. v. Carmichael, 526 U.S. 137, 119 S. Ct. 359, 142 L. Ed. 2d 324 (1999).

8   *Daubert v. Merrill Dow Pharmaceuticals, Inc., supra*, p. 589.

Under this group of cases, a conclusion or opinion qualifies as scientific knowledge if the party offering it demonstrates that it results from sound "scientific methodology" derived from the scientific method. There are offered in these decisions a set of "flexible" and "non-dispositive" general observations that may establish the validity of scientific testimony, as follows:

1. Whether the theory or technique is empirical (verifiable, refutable, or testable)

2. Whether it has been subjected to peer review and publication

3. What the known or potential error rate is

4. The existence and maintenance of standards and controls concerning its operation

5. The degree to which the theory and technique is generally accepted by a relevant scientific community[9]

In 2000 and again in 2011, Federal Rule of Evidence 702 was amended in an effort to bring it into conformity with the holdings of the Daubert cases. It now reads:

A witness who is qualified as an expert by knowledge, skill, experience, training, or education may testify in the form of an opinion or otherwise if:

(a) The expert's scientific, technical, or other specialized knowledge will help the trier of fact to understand the evidence or to determine a fact in issue,

(b) The testimony is based on sufficient facts or data,

(c) The testimony is the product of reliable principles and methods, and

(d) The expert has reliably applied the principles and methods to the facts of the case.

---

9   *Daubert v. Merrill Dow Pharmaceuticals, Inc., supra*, p. 594.

While the expert is granted automatic credibility based upon establishment of status as expert, this does not mean that the expert's opinion is automatically accepted. The trier of fact (either the jury or the judge or an arbitrator without a jury) is not obligated to accept an expert's opinion. As with any other witness, it is up to the trier of fact to ascertain whether the expert witness is believable. The jury or judge without a jury is permitted to choose to accept the expert's opinion or not. The testimony of an expert may be believed in its entirety, in part, or not at all. Juries are routinely instructed to consider such factors as the expert's level of training and experience, the facts relied on, and the reasons for the expert's opinion in evaluating expert testimony.[10]

Expert opinion is rarely given in a vacuum. Both parties (or in complex cases, almost all parties) will usually retain experts. The waggish Gibson's law states, "For every PhD, there is an equal and opposite PhD."

In jury cases, the credibility of expert witnesses is a matter for the jury to decide, after proper instruction by the judge.[11] A jury may not arbitrarily or unreasonably disregard the testimony of an expert, but it is not bound by the expert's opinion, and it is authorized to give to each expert opinion the weight that it finds it deserves. As long as it does not do so arbitrarily, a jury may disregard the testimony of a party's expert witness even though the other side has presented no contrary expert opinion.[12]

The independent professional expert adds much to the body of learning that comprises a case. In the nonexpert consultant context, professionals devote themselves to treating a patient or addressing remediation of construction defects on a client's building or preventing further soil erosion or landslide, as examples. In this connection, they are concerned primarily with resolving the patient's or client's problem. The independent expert, on

---

10   CACI, No. 219, *Expert Witness Testimony*.

11   CACI, No. 291, supra, *Williams v. Volkswagenwerk Aktiengesellschaft* (1986) 180 Cal. App. 3d 1244, 1265, 226 Cal. Rptr. 306.

12   CACI, No. 219, supra, *Howard v. Owens Corning* (1999) 72 Cal. App. 4th 621, 633, 85 Cal. Rptr. 2d 386.

the contrary, freed from preoccupation with resolving the client's problem, has a completely distinct role and is at liberty to make deliberate, sober, and detached evaluation of the condition and its causes.

The independent expert has the luxury to investigate and to make conclusions unburdened by the need to solve the underlying problem. Thus independent expert evaluation often is superior from the standpoint of objectivity. The independent expert, moreover, can examine the case from a position above preoccupation about monetary gain or prospect of recovery, which could taint neutrality.

The use of expert witnesses in law cases may date as far back as the eighteenth century in England; in 1782, a court hearing a matter concerning the silting up of Norfolk Harbor allowed the evidence of a prominent civil engineer. The use of experts has been more or less controversial ever since, but the practice has grown in scope and prevalence such that the participation of experts is ubiquitous (if not mandatory) in modern litigation.

If indeed the use of expert witnesses dates to 1782, and while a history reaching that far back in time might be thought to represent a venerable precedent for the practice, the legal system out of which expert witness practice has developed is itself significantly older. No understanding of the role and utilization of expert witnesses can be complete without at least a brief consideration of the more general history of the Anglo-American jurisprudence from which they have sprung.

CHAPTER FOUR

THE COMMON LAW:
THE HEARTBEAT OF ANGLO-AMERICAN JURISPRUDENCE

Well remembered by me is an event that occurred late in 1973, not long after my admission to the practice of law. I was invited to attend a trial postmortem between Samuel H. Berry, then the doyen of civil defense practice in Oakland, California, and his client in a case they had just finished. The jury's verdict had been for the most part favorable, and the result was considered a clear win. There had been one element of the jury's decision, however, that had gone against the client, and the discussion turned to it.

Filled with righteous indignation born of having almost entirely prevailed, the client began to grouse about the part of the case that had been lost and asked, "Now really, Mr. Berry was that justice?" Berry steepled his fingers, thought a moment, and said, "Well, sir, you went to court. You got law. If you want justice, you've got to go to God."

This comment was neither cynical nor flippant. It represented simply the very realistic understanding that the law is a system. It is an ancient, sometimes quirky, but highly developed and refined system that, like any, has its many virtues and a few faults. Professionals who undertake to develop expert witness practices need to be keenly aware of and fully schooled in the history and operation of it.

The system of Anglo-American law is essentially grounded in the Common Law, which has a long and storied history.

The Common Law originated in England in the Middle Ages. It is a system of law that has been developed by judges and juries. The underlying principle is that cases having similar facts should be treated similarly. If a similar case has previously been resolved, the current court is bound to use and follow the reasoning in the prior matter. If the current dispute is distinct from prior matters, then judges have the power to make new law by creating new precedent. The precedents are recorded in written decisions that are gathered and preserved in more or less orderly fashion. The whole body of precedent taken together is called the Common Law.

Prior to 1066 and the Norman conquest of England, justice there was carried out at the county level (then called "Shires") by the sheriff and local bishop acting in concert and between them with both civil and ecclesiastical authority. The practice of trial by jury was inaugurated in these courts. Henry II was crowned king of England in 1154 and took great interest in the English legal system. He reinstated the jury system and in essence nationalized the Common Law system by unifying it and reducing local idiosyncrasies. As a result, jury verdicts became grounded in established common mores and principles. Reliance upon formally presented evidence would be added later. Thus, in theory at least, justice was administered on the basis of law common to the entire realm.

More recently in history, nations and states have enacted written constitutions, statutes, and codes that also embody and state the law. This is typically called statutory law or regulatory law and is enacted by the various legislatures or agencies of executive branches having jurisdiction. Not surprisingly, these legislative enactments themselves have required clarification and interpretation. The courts have undertaken this again by way of written decisions, and this body of precedent forms a significant additional part of the Common Law.

Noteworthy distinction is appreciated between jurisdictions wherein the Common Law obtains and those that utilize code or civil law. In the civil law jurisdictions that comprise most of Europe, for example, the courts lack the jurisdiction to act in cases where there is no controlling statutory provision. There, judicial interpretation is considered inferior to the writings of legal scholars. Civil law countries generally trace the history of their systems to Roman law and the Napoleonic code. Common Law jurisdictions descend from England.

One of the great distinctions of the Common Law is that it eagerly grows and develops in response to the evolution of society, changing needs and developing learning and understanding. Oliver Wendell Holmes commented, "The proper derivation of general principles of both common and constitutional law ... arise gradually, in the emergence of a consensus from a multitude of particularized prior decisions."[13] Perhaps reflecting the great American penchant for pragmatism, Justice Benjamin Cardozo observed, "The common law does not work from pre-established truths of universal and inflexible validity to conclusions derived from them deductively. Its method is inductive, and it draws its generalizations from particulars."[14]

The Common Law is distinguished by its flexibility. It is free to adapt, with good and sound reasoning, to the ever-evolving philosophical, sociological, and political changes that regularly occur in daily life. In addition, the incremental development of the Common Law through multiple series of decisions that slowly (sometimes almost imperceptibly) conform the state of the law to current reality is frequently superior to legislative enactments that can be sweeping in scope, consequence, and disruption.

An additional distinguishing characteristic of the Common Law is that it is "adversarial" as opposed to "inquisitorial" (as are most civil law systems). In the adversarial construct, two or more sides present their cases to a neutral judge and jury, with the judge acting as unbiased referee. In the inquisitorial

---

13   Frederic R. Kellog. "Law, Morals and Justice Holmes," *Judicature* 96 (1986), 214–18.

14   Benjamin N. Cardozo, *The Nature of the Judicial Process* (1921), 22–23.

model, an examining magistrate fulfills dual roles of investigation of the facts and developing arguments for both sides of the presented issue. As will be seen in detail throughout this book, the adversarial nature of the Common Law has measurable effect on expert witness work.

Reliance upon the decisions of judges and juries has become one of the hallmarks of the Common Law system. That reliance, refined, cultivated, and embodied as the Common Law, has richly promoted commercial development and success in the United States. Since the Common Law amasses acceptably clear direction and predictability on a panoply of circumstances, businesspeople (as well as the public at large) enjoy a high level of confidence in determining what is legally acceptable and what is not.

The range of activities that benefit from a clear, understandable, and predictable system of law is unlimited and is borne out practically by the notable success worldwide by American business and culture. Much credit for this devolves upon the judges and juries who continually, year in and year out, engage in the laborious and slow, but exceedingly valuable, process of making the law.

The professional who intends to engage in expert witness practice is well advised to be acutely aware of the history and spirit of the Common Law. It has unusual, if not unique, infrastructure, practices, and procedures. There is special nomenclature, and occasionally common words have special "term of art" meanings. These need to be recognized and understood in their Common Law connotations. For example, the concept of "proximate cause" or "legal cause," as it is sometimes now called, has peculiar meaning and significance in the law. A detailed discussion of the concept follows in chapter 5.

Historically, moreover, as has been previously noted, the Common Law greatly predated the development of the scientific method. The law has a far different process from medicine, engineering, and the other sciences in pursuing investigation and establishing facts. The law places far less reliance on empirical evidence and far more reliance on historical method, intuition, pragmatism, and instinct than do the sciences.

From a practical standpoint, this means that professional experts, especially those whose training is in science, will be dealing with people who are good writers and talkers, but who are often poor scientists. Expert communications, especially the formal ones, are going to persons who understand and display good grammar and composition, but may not be attuned to science. As a result, communications of all types, but reports and testimony particularly, need to be well cast, evidencing good usage, cogency, and logical tightness.

Finally, for more than a thousand years, the jury has been at the center of the system and has formed the essence of it. The law relies heavily on what the judgment of twelve individuals, randomly drawn from the community at large, will be in any given set of circumstances. A very great deal of practicing law involves prediction of what a jury will do with the facts at hand. Expert witness practice is intimately and inextricably involved with the process, not only of predicting what jury outcomes will be, but also with influencing juries as well.

Since expert witnesses represent an element of modern litigation that is continually growing in significance and influence, individuals who engage in that practice, as has been seen above, are well served by acquiring a working understanding of the legal system and the various groups of people who practice it. Similarly, expert witnesses, both experienced and aspiring, will profit from a good working knowledge of legal procedure and the typical phases through which civil cases pass.

CHAPTER FIVE

THE ANATOMY OF A MODERN TORT CASE

The capacity of the Common Law to adapt and to evolve in response to the exigencies of society and commerce is likely nowhere better observed than in the development of modern tort law. "Torts" is the legal category devoted generally to personal wrongs. The purview of other categories, such as criminal law, property law, or contract law, is obvious from their respective names. "Torts" is an odd word and needs some explanation.

In ancient times, torts dealt with such basic matters as assault, battery, trespass, slander, and libel. The areas of modern personal injury and product liability law grew up through the evolution of the Common Law as extensions of traditional tort law.

Historically, damages for injury, produced as the result of contact between one person and another, were dependent upon proof that the defendant party acted intentionally. The Common Law was highly sensitive to traditions preserving individual freedom and liberty.

However, as society became markedly more complex during the Industrial Revolution, it was recognized that individual liberty could absorb restriction to the extent that a person could incur liability for acting in a careless or negligent manner. Judges and juries began to find that in circumstances in which the actor failed to exercise the level of care expected of a reasonably prudent and careful person, and when that failure produced injury to another, damages would be payable.

Also illustrative of the incremental change that results from the operation of the Common Law is the development of the doctrine of liability for the production of defective products. Originally, the state of the law was such that a person injured by a defectively made product could recover against its manufacturer only if the injured party had an actual contractual relationship with the maker. As late as the early years of the twentieth century, for example, courts held that the owner of an automobile could not recover against its manufacturer for injuries resulting from a defective wheel, as the owner's contract was with the dealer only and not with the vehicle manufacturer.[15]

Promptly, however, the rule was expanded to allow liability to extend to anyone who was damaged, as long as it was reasonably foreseeable that the manufactured item would cause injury if carelessly made.[16] Later the rule was further extended to permit recovery upon demonstration that the product was defective, regardless of whether any negligence or carelessness was involved in its manufacture.

Over the centuries, then, the Common Law slowly but surely expanded the philosophy of legal responsibility for injury to another from intent to carelessness and, finally, to "you touched it, you own it." Nevertheless, as to responsibility for carelessness, the Common Law has developed a commonsense approach and test, known as the duty of care and the reasonable man standard.

The Liability Nexus: The Duty and Standard of Care

In keeping with concerns for preservation of individual liberty, liability came to attach if an entity has a duty of care toward the injured one. Duty of care is a very broad concept, and duty can exist to almost anyone under a wide array of circumstances. Once a duty of care is established, then the conduct of the actor must fall below the standard of what a reasonably careful and prudent person would do in the same or similar circumstances.

---

15   Cadillac Motor Car Co. v. Johnson, 221 F. 801 (2nd Cir. 1915).

16   MacPherson v. Buick Motor Co., 217 N.Y. 382, 111 N.E. 1050 (1916).

Conduct at or above this standard is not negligent, and no liability attaches to it. Conduct below is negligent, and liability attaches. It is to be emphasized that the standard is that of an ordinarily reasonable and careful person of ordinary intelligence and faculties. Except in matters of professional negligence, the standard is not one contemplating any special education, training, capabilities, or ability.

Having defined the conceptual basis for the attachment of responsibility for careless conduct, a three-step process of establishing the case has developed.

A Legal Trilogy: The Elements of a Negligence Case

It is a relatively simple matter to have and maintain a claim for damages. Absent a settlement, however, a claim is not converted to money in the claimant's pocket unless a favorable verdict and judgment are obtained. Like a literary trilogy, every tort case consists of three equally significant and important stories. These are the three elements in making the typical case:

1. Liability

2. Causation

3. Damages

It is noteworthy that the court considers these elements *in this order*.[17] Then the jury is instructed to decide them in this order. They may be visualized as links in a chain extending from claim to verdict. If any one link in the chain is broken, the claim fails and the defendant prevails.

---

17   See, e.g., CACI, VF 400-402.

Liability

For the purposes of liability, duty and the standard of care vary under different types of common circumstances. Doubtless the most usual is vehicular collisions. Every driver and every vehicle owner has a duty of care to any and all persons who might be injured by their vehicle. The conduct of any driver who becomes involved in a vehicular collision is measured against that of a reasonably prudent person in the same or similar circumstances. With the modern volume of roads and vehicles, the possible permutations of the conduct of drivers who crash into each other is almost infinite. It falls to juries to determine who acted reasonably and prudently and who did not.

As to the condition of property, all owners and occupiers of property are required to keep their property free of defective conditions that may cause injury. The duty of care in the case of property defects varies depending upon what relationship the injured party has to the property itself and to its owner. In theory at least, the duty owed to an invited business patron is higher than that, for example, owed to a trespasser. Property owners are required to maintain their property free of defective conditions that they know (or should know) about. The property owner is not liable for conditions that were unknown and could not reasonably have been discovered.

Liability for the activities of animals varies from species to species, but dogs, of course, are the most common. The law has determined that the standard of reasonable care does not apply to dog-bite incidents, and owners and persons responsible for dogs as a matter of good public policy are held strictly liable (i.e., without reference to any fault) for injuries caused by dog bites and knockdowns.

Liability attaches in all matters involving intentional conduct, such as assault, battery, abuse of another person, libel, slander, conversion of property, and driving under the influence. Here the calculus shifts from duty of care to the state of mind of the defendant. Typically, proving state of mind is a higher and more difficult standard than negligence. The line between careless and intentional conduct is often blurred. Insurance only covers careless or negligent acts. In order to bring insurance in, the injured party often claims both types of conduct when the facts justify doing so.

Many expert specialties such as accident reconstruction are intimately concerned with liability issues. On the other hand, medical experts are involved with causation and damages but not liability.

Legal Causation

The next element in establishing liability is legal (or proximate) cause. Legal cause is essentially the logical bridge between liability (careless conduct) and damages. The concept is complex and difficult. It asks whether an event is closely enough related to a claimed injury so as to be reckoned as the "cause" of that injury.

An initial assessment is known as the "But For" test. If the incident would not have happened "but for" the action, then cause is established. For example, but for the defendant driver running the red light, the vehicular collision would not have occurred. However, the But For test is easily demonstrated and does not necessarily discriminate as to levels of fault. (For example, "but for the sudden thunderstorm and downpour of rain, the crash would not have occurred.") As a result, additional tests are commonly used to ascertain if an event is close enough to the resulting harm so as to constitute its legal cause.

"Foreseeability" is probably the most prevalent of these additional tests. It asks whether the damages caused were reasonably predictable in the circumstances. The type of harm is critical to this test. It is foreseeable that if a heavy object is thrown at and hits a person, injury will result. Injury is also foreseeable if the thrown object hits a piece of furniture and the furniture then falls onto and injures a person.

Additional complication is introduced, however, when more than one cause combines to produce injury. This is called "concurrent cause." The classic case involved two hunters who both carelessly discharged their shotguns in the direction of their guide. A piece of buckshot lodged in the guide's eye. While it could not be ascertained which shooter's pellet struck the guide, since both were careless, they were determined to have shared liability.[18]

Causation is frequently reckoned in terms of whether the action was a "substantial factor" in producing the alleged harm. California recently promulgated jury instructions written in modern language. The California Civil Instructions (CACI) contains the current jury instructions that are given in California on various issues. CACI 430 provides guidance in determining legal cause in terms of several considerations. A substantial factor in causing harm is reckoned as that which an ordinary and reasonable person would consider to have contributed to the harm. It must be greater and more significant than a remote or trivial factor. It does not have to be the only cause of the harm. Conduct is not a substantial factor in causing harm if the same harm would have occurred anyway without that conduct.[19]

Professional experts are frequently asked to offer opinions on the issue of causation. This can be confounding. Determining whether or not a particular effect is the probable result of a given cause starts with an understanding that the law makes of the difference between "probability" and "possibility." "Probability" in most jurisdictions is defined as being "more likely than not" or being of "greater than 51 percent likelihood." "Possibility" is anything less.

Injuries or damages allegedly resulting from an accident or incident need to be the probable result of it in order for legal probable cause to be demonstrated. Possibility is insufficient and irrelevant.

---

18   Summers v. Tice, 33 Cal. 2d 80, 199 P. 2d 1 (1948).

19   CACI 430, *Causation: Substantial Factor* reads as follows:
A substantial factor in causing harm is a factor that a reasonable person would consider to have contributed to the harm. It must be more than a remote or trivial factor. It does not have to be the only cause of the harm.
[Conduct is not a substantial factor in causing harm if the same harm would have occurred without that conduct.]

Here the difference between the scientific method and legal practice is quite stark. Science, and especially medicine, requires exploration of all possibilities to reach a "differential diagnosis." In law, the goal, and in fact the requirement, is to determine which cause and which effect are "probable," that is to say "more likely than not." At court, only the probable will be admitted into evidence.

Many evaluators, particularly medical-legal experts, fall into the trap of finding probable cause based upon the mere fact that the injury chronologically followed the event, with no other identifiable intervening cause(s). The mere fact that one event follows another chronologically does not necessarily establish legal causation. Experts should resist the practice of attributing an injury or condition to a preceding event merely because the condition arose after the event.

Mere chronological sequence does not always establish probable cause. The lack of any identifiable cause beyond the earlier occurring incident may mean that probable causation is not established. The probability that the injury resulted from the event often needs to be based on more than chronological sequence. The probability that the condition results from the symptoms presented often needs to be based on more than the lack of any alternative explanation.

The Dope on Damages

The last book in the trilogy is damages. If both liability and causation are established, then the inquiry proceeds to damages. Damages are categorized into special/economic, general/noneconomic, and punitive. By vigorously litigating liability and causation, defendants hope the jury will never reach the question of damages. Nevertheless, there may exist a duty of care, and the duty may have been breached by negligence, and the incident may have legally or proximately caused injury. But if the demanding party suffered no legally recognizable damages, there is still no recovery.

Special/Economic Damages

In personal injury matters, special damages include all medical, hospital, chiropractic, acupuncture, physical therapy, and diagnostic expenses.[20] Further, the measure of the amount recoverable is the reasonable and necessary charges paid or incurred plus those amounts reasonably probable to be incurred in the future.

The key in terms of special damages for medical care is whether they are reasonable and necessary. Expert medical testimony is greatly helpful in this inquiry.

Occasionally, injured claimants go overboard in their treatment. One plaintiff who had sustained a spinal injury in a moderately severe motor vehicle accident ultimately presented with thirty-six months of consistent and regular treatment. The various locations and modalities included emergency room charges, medical doctor visits, chiropractic visits, physical therapy sessions, aqua therapy, shiatsu massages, acupuncture, and even a few aromatherapy treatments.

The defending attorney and the retained medical expert had calendars for the months in question blown up. They then color-coded the various modalities of treatment and marked them on the calendars. Very often there were several different colors in a single week (and frequently even on the same day). This demonstrated dramatically the overlapping nature of the treatment, and the excessiveness of it was, thus, literally "highlighted" for the jury during the expert's trial testimony.

In nonpersonal injury cases (such as damage to vehicles, personal property, and real property), the measure of damages is the diminishment of value or the cost of repair, whichever is less, plus loss of use, if any.[21]

---

20   CACI 3092, *Economic and Noneconomic Damages*, and CACI 3093, *Items of Economic Damage*.

21   CACI 3903F, *Damage to Real Property (Economic Damage)*, 3903G, *Loss of Use of Real Property (Economic Damage)*, 3903K, *Loss or Destruction of Personal Property (Economic Damage)*, and 3903M, *Loss of Use of Personal Property (Economic Damage)*.

Special/economic damages also include all past loss of earnings, salary, wages, benefits, and all the same emoluments of employment that can reasonably be expected to occur in the future.[22] Also included is loss of employment capacity in the case of a claimant who may have been unemployed at the time of the incident but who reasonably expected to be re-employable in the future.[23]

Loss of earnings is often hotly contested in injury cases. Expert assistance is often critical in responding. Lost time from work adds up quickly, especially if the claiming party has a high salary with good benefits. One plaintiff who was a merchant seaman claimed a huge wage loss of some twenty-four months as a result of an accident. Under the applicable union work rules and salary agreements, this individual was paid a very high rate per day while at sea.

He implied that he had lost virtually seven hundred thirty days (two years) of pay. The defending attorney and retained forensic accountant, after examining his record of sailings in exhaustive detail, were able to determine that his true historical pattern had been to effectively remain ashore for approximately two thirds of each year. His loss of earnings claim was thereby reduced to a third of what was originally indicated.

In fatality cases, the decedent's estate may claim medical expenses prior to death, and in a separate claim, the decedent's statutorily specified heirs may claim the value of support that they would have received, had the decedent lived.[24]

General/Noneconomic Damages

This category of damages is commonly called "pain and suffering." Pain and suffering is the whole group of damages awardable for inconvenience, upset, fear, pain, indignity, disfigurement, and disruption of life.[25]

---

22 CACI 3903C, *Past and Future Lost Earnings (Economic Damage)*.

23 CACI 3903D, *Lost Earning Capacity (Economic Damage)*.

24 CACI 3921, *Wrongful Death (Death of an Adult)*.

25 CACI 3905A, *Physical Pain, Mental Suffering, and Emotional Distress (Noneconomic Damage)*.

This category also includes damages for loss of consortium. In the case of a married couple, the noninjured spouse may recover the value of the loss of the injured spouse's society, care, love, comfort, conjugal relations, and value of the injured spouse's household services.[26]

General damages are awardable in wrongful death cases to the statutorily prescribed survivors of one who is killed in an actionable incident comprising their lost society, comfort, care, love, and affection.[27]

Punitive Damages

Punitive damages are awardable in all matters wherein the conduct of the defendant is demonstrated to have been malicious, intentional, deliberately calculated to harm, fraudulent, deceitful, or in conscious disregard of the safety or rights of another. They are assessed as punishment and are designed to make an example of the wrongdoer. There is no specific measure of punitive damages, but the defendant's wealth is evidence that may be presented to the jury to assist it in reaching an appropriate figure.[28]

Additional Types of Damages

Attorney's fees are recoverable normally only in cases brought under specific statutory schemes that allow them (e.g., the Americans with Disabilities Act) or where provided by contract. Since in the vast majority of personal injury cases there is no contract, attorney's fees are virtually never available as damages in those types of cases. However, in all cases based on contractual obligations, attorney's fees can be and very frequently are a factor. Most states provide that if a contract allows recovery of attorney's fees by one party, a reciprocal provision is implied in the contract even if not specifically stated.

---

26   CACI 3920, *Loss of Consortium (Noneconomic Damage).*

27   CACI 3921, *Wrongful Death (Death of an Adult),* and CACI 3922, *Wrongful Death (Parents' Recovery for Death of a Minor Child).*

28   CACI 3940, *Punitive Damages,* et seq.

In some statutory schemes, such as the rental of residential property, double or treble damages may be available for certain damage elements. Again, multiple damages are rarely assessed in personal injury matters.

The opinions of expert witnesses proficient in one or more fields of expertise are relevant and material in each of the three elements of the legal trilogy. Accident reconstructionists, biomechanical specialists, architects, contractors, and engineers frequently become involved with and testify as to liability issues of fault, negligence, and product and construction defects. Experts in these disciplines, as well as medical professionals, are also critical in the evaluation of the intricacies of causation. Finally, the spectrum of medical specialists, forensic accountants, architects, contractors, and engineers provide invaluable insight into issues of damages.

From a chronological standpoint, civil cases go through at least three stages. These include pleading, discovery, and trial. (Appeal, as it is comparatively rare, has not been included in this list.) The pleading stage involves legal work, the goal of which is the refinement of the legal documentation that initiates the suit and responds to it. Pleading comprises the formal complaint (or petition) and the formal answer (or response), as well as legal challenges to them. Experts are involved only occasionally at this stage.

The discovery phase (discussed in detail in the next chapter) represents the formal investigation of all case particulars pursuant to court supervision and applicable court rules. There have developed several discovery vehicles through which the parties to a suit are allowed to investigate their case and to acquire access to a broad spectrum of evidence and potential evidence. Experts of all disciplines are intimately involved in discovery and in the various methods that comprise it.

Finally is the trial phase. On average, some 3 percent of cases that are filed actually go to trial. Experts are critically important in trial. The relatively low percentage of cases that go to trial does not diminish the importance of expert participation in trial. All cases are (or at least should be) worked up as if they will go to trial, so that throughout the dedication and diligence of all participants, including and especially experts, must be at the level appropriate for trial.

Workers' Compensation

All of the foregoing is to be strictly differentiated from workers' compensation cases. Workers' compensation is an entirely statutory creation enacted by governments and legislatures. It is separate and apart from the Common Law. Workers' compensation involves a sort of "Grand Bargain" by virtue of which employers are required to pay into benefit plans, usually through insurance companies.

Workers' compensation statutes provide medical coverage and temporary and permanent disability coverage to all workers injured in the course and scope of employment, regardless of fault on the part of either the employee or employer. In exchange for mandatory participation in the compensation scheme, the laws provide that the workers' compensation system is an "exclusive remedy." It is the only source of payment of benefits for damages arising from work-related injuries. Employers are insulated from any and all other liability and claims to their workers, including specifically all claims for liability for negligence.

There are boards that adjudicate disputed workers' compensation matters, but cases are nonjury, and fault is not an element of proof.

Otto von Bismarck initiated one of the earliest workers' compensation acts in Germany in 1884.[29] In the United States, Maryland passed the first comprehensive, statewide statute in 1902, and the first federal scheme covering federal employees was enacted in 1906.[30] The remaining states followed suit. The federal government provides workers' compensation

---

29 F. W. Taussig, "Workmen's Insurance in Germany," *The Quarterly Journal of Economics* 2(1) (1887): 111, 121–28.

30 The Federal Employers' Liability Act (FELA), 45 U.S.C., Section 51 et seq. (1906).

for its various classes of workers, but most schemes are still set up and administered separately on an individual, state-by-state basis.

Workers' compensation has been characterized as a "benefits delivery system," and the amount and extent of benefits varies by state. However, most schemes make provision for weekly or biweekly payments in lieu of wages, reimbursement of or direct payment of medical and related expenses, and ongoing medical expenses and permanent disability. In the case of death, benefits are paid to the survivors of the deceased worker. Pain and suffering, that is to say, general damages, are usually not paid, nor are punitive damages, except in specifically delineated and comparatively rare circumstances.

It should be noted that whereas employers are shielded from any claims beyond workers' compensation, third parties are not. Thus, in the eventuality of injury to a worker which is the result of the combined activities of the employee, the employer and another entity or entities, the worker is still at liberty to make claim against and, if necessary, to sue all others who are allegedly responsible. Third party claims and judgments are reduced by the amount of benefits collected by the plaintiff through workers' compensation.

Expert involvement in workers' compensation matters, in particular that of medical experts, is tightly controlled by statute. The selection of doctors, scope of examinations, form and contents of reports, payment, and many other matters are prescribed by law. However, third party defendants are at liberty to pursue expert assistance in the normal course of the development and workup of traditional civil litigation.

Having now explored the general outline of the civil litigation matter, we turn attention to the specifics of the discovery process.

CHAPTER SIX

DISCOVERING DISCOVERY

Anyone can investigate anything. An individual willing to devote time, effort, and money can look into such matters of interest as may be desired. Such investigation, however, is limited to the cooperation that can be voluntarily secured from witnesses and other persons of interest.

Legal discovery is a form of investigation that is done in conjunction with a pending lawsuit and under the auspices of the court and, most significantly, under the threat of possible penalty and sanction for failure to cooperate and comply.

Note that investigation can be done at virtually any time by virtually anyone.

Discovery is done only with a lawsuit pending, pursuant to which the parties are subject to the jurisdiction of the court. The processes of the court are not involved in nondiscovery investigation, but they most affirmatively direct and control discovery. There are no legal penalties for failure to participate in a general investigation, but there are penalties (potentially quite severe and possibly expensive) for failure to cooperate fully in completing discovery obligations.

Due process is an essential element of the law, and it requires that all parties be fully notified of all proceedings that affect them. Due process extends to discovery. There are generally well-defined time periods during the pendency of the case when discovery is "open," that is to say, allowed; after this, it is no longer permitted (or "closed").

The various jurisdictions have different schemes that control the discovery process. In federal courts, the Federal Rules of Civil Procedure (FRCP) form the structure and controlling authority for discovery.[31] Many states, such as Arizona,[32] Colorado,[33] and Nevada,[34] follow the FRCP more or less closely. Other states have their own separate and individually crafted discovery acts. California, for example, has its own Discovery Act that forms an integral part of its Code of Civil Procedure (CCP).[35]

Civil discovery acts govern and control the formal investigation that is done in a case after a suit is filed. They contain both limitations on the types and amount of discovery that may be done and penalties for failure to comply with its requirements.

They regulate and specify the following typical vehicles of discovery:

Scope of Discovery
Interrogatories
Depositions
Requests for Admissions
Document Demands
Demands for Production and Inspection of Things
Independent Medical Examinations
    Demand for Medical Examination
    Conduct of Examinations
    Report of Examination
Exchange of Expert Witness Information
Expert Witness Discovery and Depositions

---

31   Federal Rules of Civil Procedure, Rules 26 to 37.

32   Arizona Rules of Court, Rules 26 to 37.

33   Colorado Rules of Civil Procedure, Rules 26 to37.

34   Nevada Rules of Civil Procedure, Rules 16.1 and 26 to 37.

35   California Code of Civil Procedure, Sections 2016.010–2036.050.

Scope of Discovery

Discovery is liberal. This is for the combined purposes of reducing unexpected surprises at trial and promoting early settlement. The idea is that if all participants approach the trial fully aware of the opposition's case, it is much less likely that game playing, manipulation, and surprises will affect the ultimate trial result.

Liberality of discovery also promotes settlement, thus releasing judicial resources for other matters. The thinking is that if all sides are fully aware of the good and bad of each other's case, sober case evaluation will be promoted and cases will resolve before trial.

Federal Rule of Civil Procedure 26(b)(1) provides that parties may obtain discovery regarding any matter that is not privileged that is relevant to the claim or defense of any party including books and documents and the identity and location of persons having knowledge of discoverable issues.

Since experts participate in discovery, they need to be fully apprised of its broad scope.

There is an essential distinction between evidence that is admissible at trial and the scope of discovery allowed under the typical discovery act. The scope of discovery is much broader than the scope of evidence considered to be material and relevant for admission at trial. Discovery may normally be had in any area of inquiry that is calculated to lead to the discovery of admissible evidence. Only relevant and material evidence is admissible at trial. Admissibility at trial is a much narrower standard.

An example is hearsay. Hearsay evidence is considered to be within the scope of discovery, but it is often not admissible at trial. As a general rule, all objections to discovery are reserved to the time of trial. The principal exceptions to this general rule are if the requested discovery is not calculated to lead to admissible evidence or violates privileged information (such as the attorney/client privilege) or seeks attorney work product (described below).

The important privileges for our purposes are the attorney/client privilege and the physician/patient privilege. In very rudimentary terms, communications between lawyers and their clients and doctors and their patients are protected from disclosure in conjunction with court proceedings. There are, of course, many exceptions and qualifications. The placing of a person's medical condition into issue in a personal injury case, in most jurisdictions, creates an exception to the physician/patient privilege. It allows access by the defendant parties to the person's medical history, records, and treating doctors.

Also the work product of attorneys is largely protected from forced disclosure to the opposing side. Work product consists of materials that reflect the attorney's thinking, strategies, mental impressions, conclusions, opinions, and legal theories. Work product is allowed, for the most part, to be kept private.

Similarly, the liberality of discovery notwithstanding, communications between attorneys and their clients, unless waived, are preserved inviolate.

The liberal policy of discovery does not mean that there are no limitations. Under Federal Rule of Civil Procedure 26(b)(2), discovery may be limited by the court if it is determined that the discovery sought is cumulative or duplicative, if the information is reasonably available from another source that is less burdensome, or if the burden and expense of the discovery sought outweighs the likely benefit (taking into account the needs and size of the case).

It will come as no surprise that the scope of discovery is very often the subject of contention and disagreement among the parties and their attorneys. At trial, issues of the admissibility of evidence are resolved directly by the trial judge, who is immediately present. Judicial officers almost never supervise discovery procedures. Disputes often arise. Most attorneys effectively (if not amicably!) resolve disputes between themselves without court intervention. However, with significant frequency, depositions and other discovery proceedings are interrupted, and the intervention of the court is sought.

There is risk involved with getting the judge involved. It is an underlying and foundational assumption that all parties will engage in discovery in good faith and will effectuate the general philosophy of liberality. Virtually all discovery statutes have provisions allowing the assessment of sanctions varying in severity from monetary reimbursement for the aggrieved party all the way to termination of a persistently offending party's participation in the suit.[36]

The courts are not hesitant to award monetary sanctions, and a discovery motion will almost always result in significant payment by the losing party. While observers of discovery proceedings, such as depositions, will frequently notice loud quarreling between attorneys, much of this is "sound and fury," and there is great incentive for all participants to resolve disputes among themselves and to avoid judicial involvement.

Interrogatories

Interrogatories are formal written questions that the responding party is required to answer in detail and under oath. There are occasionally nominal limits on the number of interrogatories that can be propounded, but in practical fact the number is virtually unlimited. It is permissible to include in interrogatories a request that the responding party identify all facts that support various contentions and list all witnesses and documents in support thereof.

Defendant parties often begin their participation in the discovery process by sending out a detailed set of interrogatories requesting that the claimant parties identify all the facts that support their claims, as well as identifying corroborating witnesses and documents. The responses then form the basis for proceeding with further discovery in an organized and directed fashion.

Interrogatories are efficient and inexpensive. When carefully crafted, they can be very effective in learning the scope and details of an opponent's case. Their primary limitation is that they do not allow for follow-up questions.

---

36   See, e.g., Federal Rule of Civil Procedure 37.

Experts retained by parties do not receive interrogatories directly, nor do they respond to them. However, they are frequently asked to assist in the drafting of effective questions to be sent out to the opposition or to assist in giving accurate and correct responses to interrogatories that have been received. In addition, experts will often be supplied with the opposing party's interrogatory answers by way of providing detailed information as to the party's claims and damages.

Depositions

Any party or other person, including experts, may be called upon to give a deposition. A definition of terms is needed here. In its broadest connotation, a deposition is any statement under oath, including written statements. Written statements under oath are also known as affidavits or declarations.

The type of deposition contemplated by discovery is a statement under oath taken in person, in the direct presence of the questioning attorneys and recorded by a certified stenographer. A formal transcription of the deposition is usually prepared, and after the deponent has had the opportunity to correct any errors, it represents a complete and accurate record of the testimony offered.

Depositions are a very common, flexible, and effective form of discovery. One of the many advantages of depositions is that they are conducted in person, face to face, and follow-up questions and cross-examination are available.

Experts are frequently called upon to give depositions. Expert depositions will form the subject matter of later chapters. Experts should anticipate that there is a moderately high possibility that a deposition will be required in any case undertaken. Experts should tailor their handling of every referral with a view toward responding effectively to a deposition request. This includes general preparedness in the effective giving of depositions and specific, careful, and organized handling of the referral, including record keeping, in anticipation thereof.

As will be discussed in detail in subsequent chapters, experts are not typically compelled to give deposition testimony gratis. The side requesting the procedure commonly pays for reasonable charges of the expert for the time required to give a deposition. The retaining side usually pays for travel and preparation time.

Requests for Admissions

This discovery device consists of addressing specific requests to an opposing party to admit specified facts or the genuineness of certain documents. Any requests thus admitted become established as fact in the case. There are strict guidelines governing the form of response to requests for admissions, so as to avoid evasiveness. A party who unreasonably and in bad faith denies a proper request for admission may be liable for the assessment of attorney fees incurred by the requesting party in proving the facts at trial that should have been admitted. The amounts involved in such an assessment can be quite large. Requests for admissions must be taken seriously.

In order to be effective against the responding party, requests must be carefully and artfully crafted. When they are thusly crafted, however, the responding party then faces a significant dilemma in striking the right balance between the possibility of surrendering important issues, on the one hand, and avoiding the assessment of attorney fees if responses are too aggressive, on the other. Requests for admissions are not made to experts. However, since from the viewpoints of both the submitting and responding party, handling them can be delicate, experts may be asked to assist with developing admissions requests and/or preparing responses to them.

Document Demands and Demands for Production and Inspection of Things

These discovery tools are largely self-explanatory and very effective. They require the production of related documents, correspondence, emails, and the like. Vehicles, instrumentalities, real property, and all manner of other items are subject to being made available for viewing, inspection, and occasionally testing.

Document demands include not only the documents themselves, but the folders, tabs, and containers in which they are maintained. One client (not an expert!) was a collector of claims for a rental car company and pursued renters who had experienced damage to their rental cars but also who had not elected to take the rental car company's contractual physical damage waiver.

Predictably there was often animosity between him and the persons from whom he was trying to collect. Many cases were not amicably resolved and went to litigation. He had the habit of writing profane and uncomplimentary notes on his file jackets about the people from whom he was trying to collect. When those files went into litigation, his file jacket notes were discoverable, had to be produced, and became an embarrassment to him.

It goes without saying that experts will regularly be asked to attend, participate in, and comment on these kinds of inspections. In advance thereof, and to insure production of the correct documents or items, experts may frequently be asked to help in drafting the initiating requests.

Likewise, experts are virtually always asked to produce their own files, file jackets and tabs in conjunction with requests for their depositions. Commensurate care in file maintenance is essential.

Independent Medical Examinations

In any case wherein plaintiff is seeking recovery for personal injuries, any defendant may normally request one physical examination of the plaintiff. The one examination rule can be a hardship on a defendant when there are injuries claimed that span two or more medical specialties. Occasionally, plaintiff's attorney will agree to an additional exam or exams, but often a court motion is required. When there are multiple defendants, the situation is easier, as each can demand one examination. The medical specialties can, by agreement among the defendants, be divided up, and the plaintiff is required to comply with them all.

Usually, the examination may not include any diagnostic test that is painful, protracted, or intrusive. Some jurisdictions have a limit requiring that the examination occur within a specified number of miles of the plaintiff's residence.

Demand for Medical Examination

The defendant's demand typically must specify the "time, place, manner, conditions, scope, and nature of the examination" as well as the identity of the performing physician. Plaintiffs usually must respond to the demand, indicating whether they will comply with the demand, will comply with an exam as modified in the response, or will not comply. If the demanding defendant believes that a response modifying the original demand is unwarranted, that defendant may move the court for an order compelling compliance with the demand.

Conduct of Examination

The individuals allowed to attend and observe the exam varies widely from state to state. In California, the examinee attorney (or attorney representative) may attend and record stenographically or by audio "words to or by the examinee."[37] Many states' rules do not comment on this issue, and it is a matter of contention in some locations. Video recording may or may not be allowed, but in most states, it does not seem to be allowed.

The spirit of most discovery statutes favors liberality and requires cooperation. As a result, there usually are no definitive rules as to the scope of the inquiry that is allowed in eliciting history from the person to be examined. The demand for examination contains additional details as to what is contemplated in the examination. The examiner is well advised

---

37 California Code of Civil Procedure, Section 2032.510.

to request copies of the demand and response for additional details, for review and comment to the referring attorney if needed.

It will be no surprise that contention occasionally arises over the scope of the history that the examiner may elicit. This subject will be taken up in Chapter 10 below. In brief, however, and bearing in mind that the liability issue is not within the purview of the medical examiner's brief, doctors are encouraged to elicit as much history as possible, both as to the incident and as to past medical history. However, it is wise, if possible, to avoid conflict over history taking that imperils the completion of the examination.

If the examinee authorizes production of previous x-rays of the affected body part(s), no new x-rays are typically allowed without court order.

Report of Examination

Under most discovery schemes, the examinee may request "a detailed written report setting out the history, examinations, findings, including the results of all tests made, diagnoses, prognoses, and conclusions of the examiner."[38] If requested the report must be delivered within time limits that vary but average thirty days. Failure to produce the report risks a court motion, possible/probable monetary sanctions, and, if persistent, termination sanctions. If requested to produce a report, the examiner is entitled to receive copies of all previous reports of the affected parts by the examinee's physicians as well as any later produced reports of either previous or subsequent examinations.[39]

Exchange of Expert Witness Information

As trial approaches, a party may demand a simultaneous exchange of expert witness information. For example, in California, this demand may be made seventy days before the first trial setting. The contents of

---

38   See, e.g., Federal Rule of Civil Procedure 35 (b)(2).

39   See, e.g., Federal Rule of Civil Procedure 35 (b)(3).

the exchange are typically specified in significant detail and, again in California, the exchange itself is then due fifty days before trial.[40]

All "natural persons" whom the party expects to call as an expert witness must be identified.[41]

There exists an important distinction between the expert as consultant and as designated expert witness. A consultant advises, tutors, and provides support to the retaining attorney on a privileged basis. All communications and information developed between the attorney and the consultant are considered private and not available in any manner to the other side.

Often experts provide their most valuable contribution as consultants and are never formally designated as retained experts. Two examples are illustrative.

One case involved prefabricated redwood cooling towers that were used to cool a number of small electric generating plants. During winter, the towers would occasionally freeze, and from time to time, the weight of the ice would destroy them. The mystery was why the towers were failing to withstand loads that the design engineer indicated they could.

It developed through expert investigation at the consultant stage that redwood, unlike other species of lumber, was conventionally "full sawn." Thus a redwood four-by-four post was normally fully four inches by four inches and not the "skinny sawn" 3-7/16 inches by 3-7/16 inches of, say, a Douglas fir post. At the time, redwood was scarce on world markets, and it developed that the lumber mills that were supplying redwood for the cooling towers had taken to skinny sawing. The expert consultants determined that the diminishment of strength in the smaller posts was just enough to cause the towers to fail to perform as anticipated.

In another case, gasoline was seeping into the corporation yard of a

---

40   California Code of Civil Procedure, Sections 2034.210 to 2034.310.

41   California Code of Civil Procedure, Section 2034.210(a).

city. The yard was located at a busy intersection that had filling stations on the other three corners. Chemical analysis indicated that the culprit gasoline had been refined at a specifically identifiable refinery, but the tanks and delivery pipes and hoses at that refinery's station at the intersection repeatedly tested perfectly tight. The expert for one of the two remaining stations that belonged to another big oil company ultimately determined that the station he represented was secretly buying gasoline from the refinery whose gasoline had been identified. This was despite its affiliation with a different company. The expert then determined that his station was thus leaking the other company's product.

Both cases were quickly settled when the consultants provided these critically important findings (the findings and involvement of the experts whose work was so helpful was never made public).

The designation of expert witnesses is an important step. Upon designation, the expert loses the status of consultant, and retroactively all conversations, correspondence, and materials generated are now discoverable and subject to production by the opposition.

Upon designation, the expert's deposition will almost certainly be promptly noticed. The deposition notice will usually have an accompanying demand for production of records and files. Everything that has been created from the date of referral forward will be subject to production.

Occasionally the expert's records as to percentage of plaintiff vs. defense work, billing records, client lists, and history of work for the referring attorney and associates (and possibly insurance company client) are demanded. It is wise to be prepared for this in advance. Experts should determine in advance how this eventuality will be handled, and they should be prepared independently to defend their business and privacy information with independent legal resources. The "optics," that is to say the appearance, of the referring attorney resisting requests for disclosures of these kinds are poor.

The expert's participation in a case is a direct threat to the monetary interests of the opposing party and attorney. As a result, every creative idea

THE EXPERT EXPERT

and legal maneuver will be employed to impugn the expert and prevent or limit appearance at trial. This is often done through a series of *in limine* motions, proceedings conducted before the court that occur just as the trial is starting.

Among other purposes, attorneys endeavor to restrict or eliminate the participation in the case of their opposition's expert(s). Obviously the need for care in every aspect of the handling of every referral from the very outset is critical. The danger that all of the effort and expense of the expert's participation can be lost as the result of successful pretrial motions is real and must be borne in mind at all stages of the referral.

An exchange of reports may also be demanded.

Exchanges of formal witness information may also be requested. In them information to be disclosed in addition to the expert's name and address includes the expert's qualifications, a statement of the general substance of the expert's expected testimony, a representation that the expert has agreed to testify at trial and will be ready to give a "meaningful" deposition, as well as the expert's hourly and daily fees.[42] Failure to designate properly is potentially disastrous and usually results in the failing party's experts not being allowed to testify.

Expert Witness Discovery and Depositions

Once designated, any other party may take an expert's deposition. In geographically larger and more populous states, there are rules limiting the distance an expert may be required to travel to the deposition.[43] In smaller states, there are not. Nevertheless, the noticing party usually must pay the expert's reasonable and customary hourly or daily fee. (The daily fee is allowed only if the expert is required to be available for a full day and necessarily must forgo all other business.[44]) If the expert's fees as demanded

---

42   California Code of Civil Procedure, Section 2034.260(a).

43   California Code of Civil Procedure, Section 2034.420.

44   California Code of Civil Procedure, Section 2034.430(e).

are thought to be excessive and no accommodation is reached, a party can seek relief from the court. The designating party pays preparation and travel fees of the expert.

Experts are not parties to the litigation in which they are involved. In some instances, compelling their participation in and compliance with discovery obligations is derivative through the party for whom the expert is working. In other cases, such as subpoenas for personal appearance and production of records, the obligation to comply is direct. On occasion expert noncooperation is detrimental only to the client; in others, the detriment can be direct.

Consultant vs. Designated Expert

It is to be borne in mind that from the time of initial contact with the referring attorney, the expert is creating evidence. This includes all notes and correspondence and all facts that are remembered and recallable without documentation. The expert does not enjoy many of the protections and privileges that the attorney has.

Everything that is said, everything that is written, and everything that occurs is discoverable retroactively, once the expert is formally designated. Thus extreme awareness and caution is needed in the matter of the making of notes, the issuing of correspondence, and the gathering of physical evidence of any kind. In this connection, it can be useful to imagine, before making any note, letter, or other item contemplated for creation, that item blown up to four-feet by eight-feet poster size and placed before a jury.

There are additional discovery vehicles of a more arcane nature not appropriate for discussion within the scope of this book and which involve experts marginally (if at all). The principal and most widely used vehicles have been discussed here in some detail. It has been seen that the role of experts and their participation in them is of undeniable significance.

As has been mentioned, two of the primary rationales for the allowance of liberal discovery are the promotion of early settlement and the avoidance of surprise at trial. Since such a very high percentage of civil cases settle (some 97 percent), it may be persuasively argued that discovery laws have and continue to admirably effectuate their intended purpose, especially insofar as the process provides litigants with essential information critical to case evaluation.

Understanding the history and development of the law and of torts (and of personal injury law specifically), and having considered and described in detail the fundamentals of the discovery process whereby cases are formally investigated and prepared for trial, our attention may now turn to the steps followed in evaluating cases and assigning monetary values to them for the purposes of settlement.

CHAPTER SEVEN

THE CLAIMS CONTINUUM:
THE PROCESS OF CASE EVALUATION

Case evaluation is a process of critical importance to parties, attorneys, and judges. Much energy is expended in it. Since most (but by no means all) civil litigation claims are covered by insurance, case evaluation is of central importance to insurance professionals and executives as well. The interest in case evaluation is so great, in fact, that a primary rationale for seeking expert participation in the pretrial stage of a legal proceeding is to assist in making this process as accurate as possible.

It is noteworthy at the outset of this analysis that the assessment and assignment of case value is not empirical or scientific. It is, on the contrary, affirmatively and decidedly subjective and anecdotal. Although computerized databases have been established and successful attempts have been made to develop case evaluation software, these are only one useful tool in the entire enterprise. As a result, the art of case evaluation, for the most part, has resisted standardization and objectification.

In keeping with our understanding of the pivotal role that juries play in the administration and development of justice, ultimately the value of any case is what twelve people from the community say it is at the end of a trial. Certainly case evaluation is not made easier by the recognized fact that no two juries will respond identically to the same case. Nevertheless, the process of case evaluation is always inextricably tied to the attempt to foresee what a jury would do with the case under consideration if it went to trial.

In very blunt, if not simplistic terms, at the end of the day, a case is worth what a jury says it is worth. Nonetheless, the need to determine as closely as possible what the jury's determination will be pervades the practice of law. It is an essential question in pretrial proceedings and is always uppermost in the minds of claims handling professionals. In this connection, the participation of experts is widely sought and of inestimable value. As has been detailed heretofore, experts' opinions contribute to case understanding at all levels including liability, causation, and damages. Since experts are at least indirect and quite often direct participants in the case evaluation process, experts need to become closely conversant with it.

PEV

Case evaluation starts with pure exposure value (PEV). PEV is the full value of the claim including all injuries and all available damages. The PEV elements are the total of all special/economic damages plus general damages/noneconomic damages (pain and suffering) and punitive damages if available (infrequently). PEV does not take into account a claimant's proportion of fault.

Expert participation is fundamentally important to case evaluators in establishing PEV. Experts ideally clarify several crucial indicia including injury/injuries sustained, causation, legitimacy of medical charges incurred, time off work claimed, future medical requirements, and the legitimacy of claimed future time off work.

General Damages

Once special/economic damages are set as closely as possible and with the benefit of all resources available, general damages are determined. Traditionally, general damages have been reckoned as a multiple of some or all of the special damages.

Points of view vary (usually from the standpoint of self-interest) as to the formula to be used for setting general damages. Formerly, a very general rule of thumb in run-of-the-mill cases was three to five times the medical expenses plus wage loss. (This was thought to give roughly equal shares of the settlement or verdict to the claimant, the attorney, and the treating medical locations, and it made the claimant whole on any wage loss.)

In recent years, juries generally have become less generous in awarding general damages. The current and very general working rule among people doing civil defense work is 1.5 to 2 times the special damages.

General damages are then added to the special/economic damages, resulting in the gross evaluation figure called PEV. It goes without saying that expert involvement, in that it addresses issues relevant to general damages, such as the examinee's complaints, extent of recovery, and duration of treatment, is centrally important to the final determination of PEV.

Plaintiff's Contributory Fault

Next, reduction for fault on the part of the claimant is taken if appropriate. PEV is now reduced by the best reasonable assessment of claimant's own proportion of fault, if any, for the injury-producing event. If the claimant is determined to have been 30 percent at fault, the gross recovery is thus reduced to 70 percent net.

Here, also, expert involvement, in that it often addresses issues relevant to liability and conditions present at accident scenes, figures into to the deduction process for contributory fault as well.

Enhancements and Deductions

Finally, enhancements and deductions are made, which increase or decrease the estimated case value. All evaluations are subject to increases and decreases in value depending upon their specific circumstances. Enhancements and deductions are critical elements in case evaluation. They regularly and dramatically affect value and significantly impact the valuation process.

Some common enhancements might include that a claimant has good witness potential. A claimant with an unusually winsome personality, who is greatly articulate, or who is physically attractive is accorded a measurable advantage in case evaluation.

One very attractive plaintiff from South America fell into a large catch basin in the rain-flooded parking lot of a restaurant in Oakland, California, when she was unable to see that the protective grate had been removed. She was not significantly injured, but due to the great indignity that she suffered and her good witness potential, her case had significant enhancement value even without major special damages.

An unfavorable independent medical examination is, of course, an important enhancement. In this connection, it is noted that cases are referred to experts for *objective* evaluation. When the facts of the matter require an unfavorable report from the standpoint of the referring party, that report should be given. The accuracy of case evaluation is paramount, and accuracy is best achieved through expert objectivity.

Further, shocking, ghastly, grisly, or horrifying facts represent an enhancement. Police agencies extensively document major accidents. Professional photographers frequently appear at major accidents and make extensive photographic records of them. The value of incidents involving death or dismemberment is commensurately higher, as are matters of high public notoriety that become a cause célèbre. A radio station in Northern California conducted an on-air water drinking contest some years ago. One of the participants drank so much water that she literally drowned. The incident was closely covered in the media, and the victim's attorney secured very high compensation for her heirs.

When a defendant's conduct was intentional (such as in DUI) or the defendant is a poor witness, the potential case value increases. In reciprocation of a claimant's good witness potential adding to value, poor witness potential on the part of the responding party, along with intentional or drunken conduct, increases value.

Common deductions follow similar patterns. When a claimant makes a poor appearance or has low witness potential, value diminishes. A favorable independent medical examination with a thorough, cogent report likewise lowers value.

Factors that reflect negatively upon the claimant, such as sub rosa films depicting activity inconsistent with claimed residual injury or significant medical history of previous problems with affected body parts, are important deductions. This is so especially if claimant has not been candid about this past history. Further, significant contributory fault on the part of some other party, especially if that party is also a defendant in the case, represents justification for making a deduction.

Finally, just as a claimant's good witness potential is an enhancement, when a defendant has excellent witness potential, it is a detraction to case value and justifies a deduction.

Case Evaluation Examples

Some elementary case evaluation examples are instructive.

Example 1: In a simple rear end collision involving no fault on the part of the claimant, only soft tissue injuries resulted. Medical treatment comprised an ER visit and six weeks of chiropractic follow-up. Medical expenses totaled some $6,500, and there were two weeks off work, representing $2,500 in lost wages. Economic damages, then, are $9,000, adding medical expenses and wage loss.

General damages, computing on medical expenses of $6,500, would probably be in the $9,750 to $13,000 range. The plaintiff and defendant have equally good witness potential and are no significant enhancements or deductions.

PEV then is in the $18,750 to $22,000 range; there being no contributory fault, that is the approximate case value as well.

In this example, it is possible that expert witness participation might be sought by the defense in the form of either an independent medical examination or independent medical records review, and by either or both sides by way of biomechanical engineering evaluation or accident reconstruction.

Example 2: In a slip and fall, the claimant, who had been drinking, experienced a fractured tibia that required no surgery. The claimant is dour, cranky, and brittle. Medical expenses amounted to $20,000, and there were two months off work, representing $11,000. Here economic damages are $31,000.

Best estimates are that a jury would find the claimant 25 percent at fault for the occurrence of the incident.

General damages, considering there was no surgery, assuming a good recovery, and, again, computing on $20,000 might be set in the $30,000 to $40,000 range (probably in the lower portion due to less than stellar witness potential). PEV then is something in the $61,000 to $71,000 area. Applying a 25 percent deduction for contributory fault, a case value is yielded in the $45,750 to $53,250 range.

The defense would doubtless seek an independent medical examination. In fracture cases, residual injuries are always of concern, even when there has been a good recovery. The plaintiff is likely to use the treating physician(s) for medical expert opinion and assistance. Both parties will likely consider accident reconstruction and will engage engineering experts to evaluate the incident and the surface (coefficient of friction, etc.) where the incident occurred.

Example 3: In this example, claimant, who before the accident was a lumbar surgery candidate but who had foregone the procedure, slipped and fell in a rain-wet business entryway. Claimant's low back condition was measurably aggravated, and now claimant has had the surgery. Medical expenses were $150,000 and loss of wages is $20,000.

Claimant is an energetic, cheerful, and optimistic person who is candid about not having been as careful as was appropriate, but the representatives of the business come across as callous and indifferent. Contributory fault is estimated at 30 percent.

Economic damages in this example are $170,000. Formulas are less applicable in bigger cases. However, considering the claimant's significantly better witness potential than the defendant's representatives, general damages computed on medical expenses of $150,000 might be in the $225,000 to $300,000 range, so that PEV is in the range of $395,000 to $470,000. Deducting for contributory fault case value might be in the range of $276,500 to $329,000.

In this last example, the defense will certainly engage one or more medical experts, as will the claimant. A full spectrum of expert workup on the scene by both sides will almost certainly be done.

Knights of the Roundtable

On the defense side, the practical process of case evaluation often occurs in what are commonly called "roundtable" discussions. Formal roundtables occur approximately monthly. They last a full day and involve the gathering of attorneys and claims professionals, supervisors, and managers. Participants often number over twenty. In order to get through the agenda, lunch is usually brought in. Hundreds of years of combined experience are applied to the evaluation process. Cases with an impending trial date, unusual fact patterns, serious or difficult to define and quantify injuries, as well as matters with high potential settlement value, are typically selected for the group's scrutiny.

As a point of departure, cases are summarized by the handling attorney and then discussed by all in minute detail. The facts of the incident are reviewed with utmost thoroughness. All of the elements of damages, special/economic and general/noneconomic, are considered. The reasonableness and necessity of treatment and the cost thereof, as well as wage loss, are fully explored. The discussion of the witness potential of the respective parties and witnesses is intense. PEV is established and case and settlement value ranges are determined. The highest degree of accuracy is sought.

The involvement of experts is an integral element of the roundtable process. If a case already has experts, they are discussed at length. Their reputations for learning, report writing ability, promptness, reliability, and ability to provide good deposition and trial testimony are commented upon. It is difficult to overemphasize the role that experts play in roundtable discussions. All participants are expected to offer their own personal observations and experiences with each expert. Comments and anecdotes about past performance are sought, shared, and received with great interest.

If there is no expert yet retained if or additional experts are needed, their selection is the subject of much additional discussion. Any needed experts will likely be chosen at this time. Names are proposed and reacted to. A very frequent statement heard as to an expert that some participants may not already know is that the expert "writes a great report." Past reputation for cooperation and collaboration in scheduling and administrative matters is always of interest. The candidate experts' histories of giving quality deposition and trial testimony are discussed and noted.

The practical lesson for experts from the roundtable process is that experts are continually making their reputations. Regardless of the level of involvement, their participation in any case will be reviewed, dissected, and commented upon intensely. All experts should proceed in every matter in accordance with this knowledge and in recognition that roundtables represent significant opportunity to become known as a desirable choice and to be more frequently retained.

The Claims Continuum

The Claims Continuum graph is a distillation of lessons learned from years of experience in claims evaluation. It demonstrates that claims become more difficult to resolve, require more intensive effort, are riskier, and are more expensive for both sides as more time elapses. Further, the continuum tracks how the rate of resolution steadily diminishes over time.

The frequency and difficulty of resolution paths cross in the Discovery and Mediation phases. This is notably well within (but somewhat toward the end of) the several phases in which medical and other experts are retained and begin their work. Expert depositions will, for the most part, not have been taken by this stage, however.

The Claims Continuum Graph

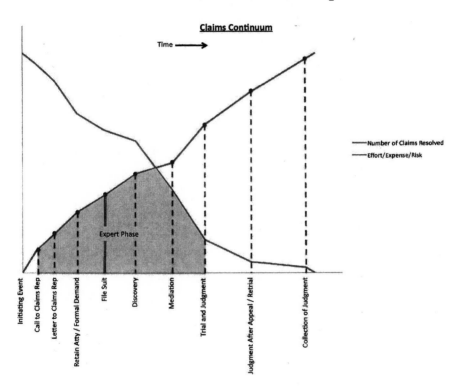

From the point of view of adjusting and defending claims, insurance companies correlate their expense and risk over time with the cost benefit that they receive from contesting or litigating claims. These graphs look very similar and insurance expense/risk cost/benefit paths cross at essentially the same juncture that they do in the Claims Continuum presented here. (In cases that have exposure for attorney's fees, the crossing point is significantly earlier.)

The Claims Continuum graph indicates that a very high proportion of claims are resolved by end of the Mediation phase. The claims that go further are exponentially more expensive, risky, and labor intensive for both sides. This is corroborated by the observation that accomplished claimant attorneys generally will settle their strong liability, high value cases. Recognizing that there is comparatively little to lose and potentially much to gain, they often will try poor liability high damages matters. This results in intense preparation by both sides, with commensurate expert witness participation.

The Claims Continuum graph also clearly demonstrates that the opportunity for experts to be retained on matters and to undertake useful and effective efforts for their clients exists primarily through the critically important first two thirds of a case's potential life. Expert participation is usually an instrumental factor in bringing most matters to successful settlement and conclusion within the time that it is most cost effective to do so.

It should be evident from this discussion that effective expert participation is an integral element of accurate claims evaluation. Regardless of whether a case goes into the stage of expert discovery, not to mention trial, expert participation at all times is of seminal importance to all stakeholders in the claims handling process.

The vast majority of cases in which experts participate have insurance policies involved for one or more of the participants. Insurance policyholders pay for coverage that not only indemnifies them (if they are subjected to a claim or suffer a judgment) but also pays for attorneys to defend claims and suits. Included in the coverage for defending claims and suits is coverage for expert witness expense. Insurance companies, then, are very often paying expert witnesses, as part of the coverage offered to their insured policyholders.

The relationship between the insured policyholder and the insurance company can be complicated. It has surely been the subject of mountains of litigation in the modern era. Since insurance is an integral consideration in so much civil litigation, experts should have a rudimentary understanding of the additional dynamics that the presence of insurance has on civil litigation. Also important are the effects of the interplay between insureds and their insurance carriers.

Stated another way, every professional expert will very likely at one time or another be a beneficiary of insurance money. This happens directly, by way of payment from defense attorneys or insurance claims departments. It also happens indirectly, assuming that the claimant's case has been successful, as the claimant's expert is paid out of the verdict that is most often itself paid by insurance money. Therefore, a basic understanding of insurance and insurance policies is in order.

CHAPTER EIGHT

PARTY DOWN!
MANAGING RISK AND REDUCING EXPOSURE:
A PRIMER ON INSURANCE

Insurance companies, through the collection of premiums, gather together and then, through indemnity and loss adjustment payments (including investigation and adjustment costs, attorney fees, and expert fees), redistribute vast sums of money each year. It is estimated that in 2010, the Unites States tort system cost totaled $264.6 billion, or $857 per person in the country.[45] Out of that, medical expert costs including independent medical examinations and related services were estimated at $4 billion.

Insurance policies in their simplest conception are contracts between the insurance companies and their customers, whereby the company agrees for a premium to make the customer whole if a loss is suffered, *up to a certain agreed upon limit.*

Policy limits are a critical limitation in insurance contracts, and they are taken very seriously. All insurance contracts have them. No policy is deliberately open-ended, and companies are careful about managing and knowing the full measure of their total exposure or risk at all times. In addition, companies are required to maintain reserves of money to pay claims in the event of a catastrophe, so they very carefully evaluate risk and exposure. They are also careful about limits for the purposes of reserves as well.

---

45   Towers Watson, *2011 Update on U.S. Tort Cost Trends*, p. 3.

Policy Limits

Single and Combined Limits: In casualty policies such as automobile, homeowners, and commercial policies, it is typical to reckon policy limits in terms both of single and combined limits and to set a maximum exposure separately for each category. These are usually denominated as "Each Person" and "Each Occurrence" limits.

Thus an auto policy might have an "Each Person" limit of $100,000. This means that the total that would ever be paid for any one person as the result of any one loss would be $100,000; there might also be an "Each Occurrence" limit of $300,000. Thus the total amount that would ever be paid to any number of people injured in that accident would be $300,000. This is commonly called a "100/300" policy.

For example, in a serious, multicar, multi-injury pile-up, a 100/300 policy would never pay any one person more than $100,000. It could pay three people $100,000 each, if all three were badly hurt. However, if the number of claims were in excess of three, and they all varied in severity, there would be no limit to the number of claims paid, but the grand total would not exceed $300,000, and no single claim would be paid over $100,000. Such instances are not unusual, and there can occur much squabbling among the several injured parties over dividing the policy limits.

In larger policies, both personal and commercial, the policy limit is frequently reckoned as an aggregate limit, perhaps of $1,000,000. This means that the company will not pay more than the policy limit for any one or more claims arising out of a single occurrence.

The various states have minimum policy limits for automobile insurance. The 15/30 policy is typical. Common nonminimum limits are 30/60, 50/100, 250/500, and 500/500. As limits increase, so do premiums. Most people pay for limits commensurate with the level of assets that they have to protect.

First Party vs. Third Party Coverage

Uninsured and underinsured motorist (described in detail below), collision, comprehensive, fire, property, theft, and underinsured property damage coverage and limits are called "first party" coverage.

Liability coverage and corresponding limits are called "third party" coverage.

This nomenclature is reckoned from the standpoint of the insurance company or carrier, which may be thought of as the "second party." The insured person (or entity), in older contractual forms, was denominated "the party of the first part," and the company "the party of the second part." The insurance contractual relationship is between those two parties. Many coverages, such as automobile collision and comprehensive and homeowner fire and other perils coverage, benefit the insured party or first party. These are called first party coverages and claims made under them first party claims.

Parties outside the immediate insurance contractual relationship may make covered liability claims. As third parties, outside the contract, their claims are referred to as third party claims.

First party claims are far more delicate, in that they involve entities that have a direct contractual relationship with each other, and who as a result of that relationship owe a higher level of good faith and fair dealing to each other.

Uninsured Motorist and Underinsured Motorist Coverage

Uninsured Motorist (UM) Coverage: Depending upon the exact locality (the percentage is higher in more heavily populated areas), 20 to 25 percent of all drivers are uninsured for automobile liability. Most if not all states require that each automobile policy offer Uninsured Motorist Coverage.

This is first party coverage, directly between the insurance carrier and its insured. It covers the driver and occupants of the insured party's own car if the adverse driver is uninsured. Coverage limits work exactly like they do in liability coverage and are usually the same as the liability amounts. Amounts different from the liability amounts may be ordered, however, and UM coverage may be waived, but a significant amount of documenting paperwork is required in order to do so.

Underinsured Motorist (UIM) Coverage: If an insured motorist is involved in an accident with someone who has liability coverage but it is coverage with lower policy limits, and if an injury results in excess of the at fault party's lower limits, there is first party coverage called Underinsured Motorist Coverage. UIM extends coverage under the person's own policy in an amount from the insufficient lower limits up to the higher ones.

Thus, if a driver has an accident with a person with a 15/30 policy and is badly enough hurt to collect that entire limit, and if that injured person has a 100/300 policy of their own, that insured then enjoys the $85,000 of underinsured first party coverage remaining under their own policy.

The Implied Covenant of Good Faith and Fair Dealing and Insurance Bad Faith Claims

The courts imply into each and every contract that is made a provision that is called the Covenant of Good Faith and Fair Dealing. While this implied clause is not actually written into the formal contract document, it is of absolutely full force and effect, and it requires that neither party will do anything to injure the rights of the other or to prevent the other from getting the full benefit of the contract.

With respect to insurance policies, this means that every insurance company is required to act in good faith toward its policyholders and treat their interests as equal to the company's own. Insurance companies may not unreasonably deny a claim or delay the payment of a claim without reasonable cause.

Part of the insurance company's good faith obligation is to fully, fairly, and without delay investigate and settle all first party claims. Retention of various sorts of experts including medical experts and the making of requests for independent medical examinations is an integral part of the carrier's good faith obligation to fully investigate an insured's claim. Heavy reliance is placed on experts to objectively and expeditiously, to the best of their professional ability, assist in carrying out these good faith obligations.

Policy Limits Demands

Claimant parties and their attorneys frequently demand the entirety of the policy limits available. This is called a "policy limits demand" (PLD). PLDs are of course for the full amount of the policy limits available and may be made in both first and third party matters. They routinely are time limit demands. There is no specifically prescribed number of days, however. General (but not universal) practice is thirty days.

Attorneys and claims representatives are routinely called upon to make case evaluations with the potential that policy limits might be exhausted. Obviously, if policy limits are paid on a case that does not warrant it, indemnity money is wasted. On the other hand, there are severe penalties for failure to pay claims within the policy limit when appropriate.

Offers of Judgment

The prevailing party in a lawsuit that goes to trial is entitled to some basic litigation expenses. These basic costs do not include the expense of expert witnesses. Nevertheless, state statutes often set up a special procedure whereby any party may make a formal settlement demand or offer of judgment (or settlement). If the verdict is better for that party than the offer, the court may, and usually does, award significantly more types and classes of costs, *including expert fees and expenses.*

This provision of the law, when utilized effectively, makes going to trial significantly more risky for all parties. The participation of expert consultants is very costly for both sides. Cost bills submitted by defendants who bettered their statutory offer of judgment have been regularly seen, especially in small cases, to exceed the amount of a small to moderate jury award. Plaintiffs often have wound up owing the defendant and defendant's insurance carrier money, the verdict in their favor notwithstanding. Insured defendants are typically covered by their policies for these costs if the plaintiff betters a statutory offer.

The investigation and opinions of experts, especially of medical experts in personal injury cases, are critical factors in attorney and insurance company evaluation of offers of judgment. They are also critical in determining whether to issue a counter offer of judgment and, if so, in what amount. Ironically, the better the work of the expert consultant, the more likely the other side will end up having to pay for it!

Offers of judgment and policy limits demands almost always have time limits (usually thirty days) in which they must be met, or the consequences of failure to do so accepted. Attorneys and claims representatives are routinely called upon to respond to them under intense time pressure and in the face of the potential that policy limits might be exhausted.

Receipt of either an offer of judgment or a policy limits demand results in the marshalling and deployment of extensive resources. This includes witness investigation, sub rosa surveillance, social site research. Most significantly of all and if not done already, the retention of medical and other expert consultants is agreed upon and initiated. As needed demands for independent medical examinations or requests for independent medical records reviews are issued.

Case evaluators very frequently refer cases to experts for assistance in determining if claims are "policy limits" or for assistance in evaluating offers of judgment. They rely heavily on the skill, ability, and expertise of their experts in so doing. These are decisions that have to be gotten right, and thus case evaluators are willing to invest heavily in the expert witness process when these decisions arise.

Insurance Bad Faith

Any failure by an insurance company to fully carry out its obligations of good faith and fair dealing constitutes a violation of the insurance agreement. Failure to comply with the good faith requirements of a policy, not surprisingly, is called bad faith. Bad faith is actionable by the insured party against the company.

Bad faith is contractual and, at least, conceptually can occur only between the actual parties to a contract. For that reason in most states it is limited to first party claims only (i.e., UM/UIM, comprehensive, first party homeowner's, and similar claims).

Types and amounts of damages available to an aggrieved policyholder increase proportionally with the egregiousness of the company's conduct. Damages for innocent, inadvertent failure to pay a claim are merely the amount originally payable under it. If the denial or delay is unreasonable, in addition to the original amount of the claim, all economic damages such as lost time are available. Damages for emotional distress and attorney's fees might also be payable. Lastly, if the conduct is outrageous, malicious, or fraudulent, then punitive damages may be sought and awarded.

Claimant parties can be quick to allege bad faith. Ongoing, collegial, congenial professional relationships (normally the essential stuff of good business) between individual attorneys and insurance companies and their "favorite experts" can lead to charges of lack of objectivity and even claims of conspiracy to harm the interests of policyholders. Strict neutrality and documentable, verifiable arm's-length relationships must be maintained between experts and those who retain their services.

As has been described in the Introduction the ability to work closely on cases with experts is always to be cultivated. However, in terms of activity outside the strict confines of individual cases, all appearance of undue influence, impropriety, working hand in glove, and any manner of coziness is to be assiduously avoided.

Unreasonable Failure to Settle within Policy Limits

As indicated, conceptually, bad faith is a first party matter. Some states allow direct third party claims against insurance companies when third parties feel that the first party's insurance company has not treated them fairly. Most states do not allow direct third party bad faith claims, however.

In either event, since the insurance company in third party matters exclusively controls the defense and settlement of those matters, a potential conflict of interest is created in cases where the claim is close to, at, or exceeds the policy limit. In such instances, the insurance company is obligated to settle within the policy limits, if it has the reasonable opportunity to do so. Having potentially exhausted its policy limit, the company is not allowed to gamble with its insured's money over the policy limit by failing to settle and to terminate the claim.

In those eventualities in which the company feels that the matter is not a policy limits one and it declines to settle within the policy, the law considers that the company has opened or uncapped the limits of the policy, and the limits are disregarded. Management views the uncapping of limits and all forms of extra contractual (in excess of policy limits) payment with consummate concern and seriousness.

Even in jurisdictions where there is no direct third party bad faith, an insured who feels that the insurance company has wrongly failed to settle within the policy (or committed some other bad faith in conjunction with the handling of a third party claim) can assign any first party claim to the claimant, thereby in effect converting the first party bad faith into third party bad faith.

In summary, the expert investigation and evaluation process has a central role in case evaluation. The misevaluation of cases can lead to multifarious difficulties for insurance companies and their attorneys. These misevaluations include unreasonable failure to settle within policy limits, the uncapping of policy limits, first party bad faith exposure, and (by assignment of rights) what might in effect be described as third party bad faith. The need for care, accuracy, skill, and independence cannot be overemphasized.

Across the entire spectrum of expert participation in a lawsuit, the matter of communication is critical. As had been detailed above, experts need to have full and unfettered access to their retaining attorneys. Experts must also have clear lines of communication as to the scope of their assignment and the many details of carrying it out. Since the majority of cases into which experts are called resolve before the expert is deposed and before trial testimony is required, the expert's report is the single best opportunity for superior communication.

The characteristics and principles of excellent report writing will now occupy our attention.

CHAPTER NINE

REPORTING FOR DUTY:
THE ESSENTIALS OF WRITING A GOOD EXPERT REPORT

Expert participation in a lawsuit might be likened to the construction of a house. In basic terms, there are three stages of building and three corresponding stages for the expert. First is the stage of laying the foundation. In this stage, the expert conducts a thorough professional investigation and, if required, writes a report that forms the basis (literally, the foundation) for further participation in the case. Next is the framing of the structure. In this phase, based upon the solid foundation now laid, the expert offers deposition testimony that is organized, structured, and suitable for the support of future work if necessary. Finally, there is the finishing of the house, with flourishes that are not only durable but also pleasing to the eye. This, of course, corresponds to testimony offered at trial before the jury that is firmly grounded in all the work that has gone before and gives all that has been done its final form and finish.

In this chapter, we will consider the all-important foundational matter of initiating and conducting a proper investigation and preparing a good report.

Eliminating Potential Conflicts of Interest

The first order of business upon contact by the referring party is to eliminate any conflict of interest. Expert witness work should not be undertaken without establishing, from the very outset, an effective procedure for identifying current and previous assignments that may represent conflict.

Little is more frustrating for the referring party or embarrassing for the expert than to be reminded well into the case that consultation has been previously made or some minor work done in the matter by the expert before the current contact. If the conflict goes unrecognized into the deposition or trial stage of the litigation, the results of discovering a latent conflict can be catastrophic, including disallowance of the expert's participation at a time when it is too late for the client to find and retain another.

Investigation and Research

The standard and complete investigation, examination, protocols, or survey that is professionally recognized and prescribed in the expert's field of specialty must routinely be completed to the best of the expert's ability. All elements of a full investigation should either be completed or justifiably deferred. If one or more elements is omitted, the expert can expect later to be cross-examined on the elements recognized by the profession in question and then impugned for not having completed them all. This is so regardless of the fact that it may have been superfluous, practically speaking, to have done one or more particular items.

It is not uncommon that either circumstances or opposing parties will contrive to prevent a full examination or investigation. Chapter 10 is devoted to the question of contention and obstruction of experts in their efforts to complete their work, and reference is made to it.

Suffice it to say here that whenever the opposing attorney or party frustrates the completion of all elements of a full investigation or examination, the details should be documented and set forth fully in the expert's report. That the opposing party frustrates some portion of the full completion of every element of a thoroughly complete professional investigation is not usually fatal to the expert's assignment. In the end, these kinds of tactics typically will redound to the detriment of the ones engaged in them. Such conduct is far more likely to prejudice the perpetrator than the party whose investigation is sought to be impeded.

The obtaining of a history is always critical and foundational. The full details of the subject incident, accident, or event should be sought and recorded with appropriate chronological details and all other relevant facts. For example, vehicle velocities and damages, site and scene particularities and peculiarities, safety measures taken or not taken, helmet and seat belt usage, and specific aftermath conditions at relevant locations (when appropriate) must be ascertained.

In medical and many other types of cases, a complete history of the patient or site is needed. Details of all previous injuries or damages and the history of exposure to relevant causes and conditions should be explored. Whether it is prior illnesses and conditions, previous water intrusion events or floods, or the history of soil settlement (to mention only a few examples), the expert must use professional experience and imagination to think of, and then inquire into, all history that could be relevant to the investigation.

Similarly, a careful exploration of events after the subject incident should be made. The course of medical treatment and its effectiveness or the progress of physical damages to property is explored. All efforts at repair and mitigation, and the identities of all practitioners, contractors, and other experts who have been involved are of interest and should be sought and recorded.

It is useful to know (when allowed) from the claimant or plaintiff what was complained of initially and the circumstances of discovery of the loss. Often claimant parties will comment on their own view of what occurred and their course of treatment or the repair of damages. They occasionally will declaim as to what they believe is wrong and what needs to be done to rectify it. If offered or allowed, this information should be taken and documented.

The effects of the incident on the person(s), site, or property of the claimant should be explored, including nature and extent of treatment, costs of repair, ancillary expense, residual physical complaints, disfigurement, disruption of activities of daily living, or loss of use of property as is appropriate.

In most referrals, there will at some time be exchanges of interrogatories and depositions as well as document demands and responses. Depending upon the time of referral, these may have been done previously or will be soon completed. Copies should be requested and studied. These types of answers to discovery often will contain significant background information. This information can be especially important if efforts have been made to impede the expert's direct exploration of the case history.

In addition, it is common, prior to the initiation of litigation, for the claimant attorney to submit a comprehensive demand letter or brochure setting forth the claim in significant detail. Regularly these documents, in addition to explaining the claim at great length, have attached to them supporting documentation of significant interest. Likewise, as and when the case has progressed to the stage of arbitration or mediation, the opposing party will submit a detailed legal brief to the arbitrator or mediator that will also have attachments of significance and interest. Referring attorneys often fail to realize that these latter types of documents will be of assistance to the expert. The expert should routinely request them.

As appropriate, most often in personal injury cases, medical and employment records of the opposing parties should be acquired and reviewed by the expert. These will, of course, always be sought in conjunction with independent medical examinations, but they are regularly useful to practitioners of other professions such as biomechanical engineers and accident reconstructionists. (Experienced litigation attorneys agree that more useful information is generally contained in and gleaned from medical records than any other source of discovery—even more than from interrogatories and depositions. Medical records are a resource for many experts that is not to be missed.)

With the advent of digital photography and the ease with which digital pictures can now be utilized in audiovisual presentations, photography has gained exponentially in importance in expert witness practice. Full photographic documentation of scenes, instrumentalities, and objects is essential. Tape measures and other objects can be very effectively used to illustrate scale. Photos assist in and corroborate the recording of measurements.

As the initial investigation phase is just that, investigation, the expert is usually free within the boundaries of professional propriety to increase the opportunity to observe the persons and conditions involved outside the strict confines of the physical examination or site/vehicle inspection. Arriving early and staying on after the formal procedure can lead to observations of interest. Watching a patient's activities beforehand at the inspection/examination location or observing interaction with friends or relatives afterward can lead to relevant information.

Formal Examination and Demand Process

Independent medical examinations, formal site inspections, and the production of vehicles and items for inspection and testing are usually initiated by formal notice. These notices specify the time and place of the examination or inspection. Additional information is required for independent medical examinations as has been discussed in detail in chapter 6 above.

Generally a one examination rule applies. It applies in practice if not by statute. This rule is observed most closely in conjunction with independent medical examinations. As has also been described in chapter 6, the one examination rule can be a hardship on a defendant when there are injuries claimed that span two or more medical specialties, but there are strategies available to address this eventuality when it occurs.

As it does not involve the examination of a person, the entire inspection process for land, buildings, vehicles, and other locations and items is often more relaxed.

Site views of the location where a slip and fall occurred are common.

Often coefficient of friction testing is done. In some instances, the defendant party whose property is being analyzed will have already asked its expert to conduct this kind of evaluation and testing beforehand. In that eventuality, the plaintiff expert completes testing alone. The defendant expert who has already done the same testing will then have the opportunity closely to observe the plaintiff expert's activities and to point out any deficiencies. At other times, circumstances will dictate that all parties conduct their testing and observation at the same time, and in those cases, the expert has dual roles of investigator and observer.

In construction defect matters, site inspections of a large commercial building or residential project can be multiday affairs attended by dozens of attorneys, parties, and experts. Again experts will usually both investigate and observe at these proceedings.

Vehicle inspections and the inspection of other types of items, physical evidence and instrumentalities are less complicated. Most often they encompass only the viewing, photographing, and measuring of the item produced. Often enough, however, there can be disassembly and testing of items or component parts. These types of inspections need to be worked out carefully in advance so that the chain of possession of components and the full participation of representatives of all parties is allowed.

From time to time, the item(s) inspected will not survive the inspection and testing intact. This is called destructive testing. The attorneys, with the help of the expert consultants, work out a protocol for the testing process and disposition of any surviving parts or components. Obviously, great care to observe all elements of the established protocol is required, and every effort to anticipate problems and potential disagreements must be made in advance.

There are no definitive rules as to the scope of inquiry that is allowed with respect to independent medical examinations in eliciting history. This subject occasionally becomes an area of disagreement. A full discussion is set forth in the next chapter on dealing with contention.

Copies of the demand and response should be provided to examiners for additional details and their review and comment. In completing a credible and complete investigation, close coordination with the referring attorney will facilitate the process, and experts should feel free to discuss concerns or request any additional information needed.

Effective Report Writing

As noted above, the report is the underlying and foundational expert activity, from which good success throughout the assignment will then spring. It should be added that an expert who can produce consistently complete, well-written, and thoughtful reports will reduce the frequency with which testimony is required, at deposition or at trial. When produced to the opposition, reports that are clear and convincing, and that cover intelligently and completely all issues, present fewer opportunities for opposing counsel to raise questions. They also stand as a discouragement from the supposition that there might be anything to gain from requiring live testimony and cross-examination.

Furthermore, it is by way of the report that an expert has most frequent and immediate contact with attorneys, judges, and insurance representatives who are active in the litigation business. Good reports are the most readily available means of establishing, fostering, and preserving an excellent reputation among the legal community.

In all cases of medical examinations, a detailed report is required if requested by the examinee. Most states prescribe an outline of the elements that the report must contain.[46] Under typical provisions, the examinee may request "a detailed written report setting out the history, examinations, and findings, including the results of all tests made, diagnoses, prognoses, and conclusions of the examiner."[47]

There is a time limit within which the report must be produced. If

---

46   See, e.g., California Code of Civil Procedure, Sections 2032.610 to 2023.650.

47   See, e.g., California Code of Civil Procedure, Section 2032.610(a)(1).

requested, the report commonly must be delivered within thirty days after demand for it.[48] Failure to produce the report risks a court motion, possible/probable monetary sanctions, and, if persistent, termination sanctions.

Interestingly, under the California statute and in many other states' statutes, if a report is requested, the examinee may also request copies of all other reports of earlier examinations of the same condition made by the examiner or other anyone else.[49] If examiners are requested to produce a report, they are entitled to receive copies of all previous reports of the affected parts by the examinee's physicians as well as any later produced reports of either previous or subsequent examinations.[50]

While reports by experts other than medical may be required less often, they still are frequently required, and the nonmedical expert needs to develop a high level of skill in producing them.

There follows a detailed analysis of the elements and characteristics of high-quality reports that will be gratefully received by parties, attorneys, and insurance representatives. This analysis will secure the expert's reputation with judges and will stand as the foundation for all further work in the matter including deposition and trial testimony. The stock in trade of the professional expert is quality opinions. The well-written report, in short, documents and secures the credibility and believability of those opinions.

Furthermore, the profusion of trial court delay reduction acts notwithstanding, there often is significant time that elapses between the expert's investigation, examination, and report and later depositions and trial testimony. The quality report, which covers all elements and which is crafted in logical and cogent terms, serves to eliminate the potential risk of loss of memory and connectedness between the intensity of the initial investigatory activity on the file and later proceedings.

---

48 See, e.g., California Code of Civil Procedure, Section 2032.610(b).

49 See, e.g., California Code of Civil Procedure, Section 2032.610(a)(2).

50 See, e.g., California Code of Civil Procedure, Section 2032.640.

General Guidelines

Before turning to a suggested outline for the excellent report, some general guidelines are appropriate. Just as all established practices of the expert's professional discipline are followed strictly in the investigation phase, these so-called best practices are also followed in generating the report. The report is the vehicle by way of which the whole of the expert's investigation reflects and documents the applicable profession's disciplinary particulars.

At the report stage, the expert needs to make careful assessment of the report's audience. As has been described above, the large majority of those who will read, study, and have the benefit of the report are individuals trained more in language and history than science. Reports should be constructed using correct grammar and usage and complete sentences. They need to be endowed with well-crafted paragraphs that employ quality topic sentences and are not excessively long. Insider shorthand and abbreviations are to be avoided.

With the advent of word processing programs, an interesting dynamic has arisen between dictating and the direct typing of reports. Each offers its advantages and disadvantages. For example, many attorneys who in their early careers became accomplished dictators have found in the current era that direct typing has many organizational advantages and promotes clarity of writing.

It is useful to ensure that reports set forth a clear and understandable introduction and that paragraphs are well organized. Each paragraph should begin with a clear topic sentence. Logical and persuasive conclusions can then be offered. Frequently reports are received by recipients who at the moment may not have the luxury of time to read and study them at leisure and in detail. Attention can be profitably given to structuring reports so that their essence can be readily gleaned in such circumstances. Whenever possible, the substance of the report should be discernable from reading the introduction, the paragraph topic sentences and conclusions.

Report Outline

The general outline of a good report is as follows:

- introduction

- report of examination

- history and material reviewed

- conclusion/impression

- discussion/explanation

The credible report starts with the introduction. Here, a succinct and summary recapitulation of the assignment, the expert's investigation and its elements, the essential facts of the examination or site inspection, and materials reviewed is set forth. The introduction can effectively be thought of as an adoption of the journalistic who, what, where, when, and why model in recitation of the assignment.

The next element is a fully detailed exposition of all examination, testing, and analysis completed. Here, the protocols followed and the observations made are set forth in detail. At this point, the ability to describe highly technical matters in simple words and to infuse a level of interest and excitement is to be cultivated.

After describing the examination, the report goes on to detail the history of the patient, location, vehicle, or site involved. It also recites all materials studied, such as medical records or other documentation and discovery, which have been reviewed and relied upon.

There then follows the conclusion, impression, diagnosis, and causation opinions. Here is the synthesis of all the facts developed, the observations made from the examination or inspection process, the findings, and the conclusions reached. In short, here the expert describes what it all means.

The causation analysis in any expert report, and especially in independent medical reports, is of central interest to its recipients and readers. As has been elucidated, causation is one of the required elements of the proof of any case, and those on the legal side are intensely interested in it. The causation question is one that is put to the jury for determination. Causation is a subject upon which experts are permitted and even encouraged to opine. Much depends on the quality of the expert's persuasiveness on the issue and on the credibility, forcefulness, and integrity of the expert's argument.

The causation opinion should be set forth confidently and without equivocation. By virtue of learning, training, and experience, the expert is entitled legally to offer the causation opinion. This should be done with clarity and conviction. Equivocation, the listing (at least at this location in the report) of other possible alternative causes, and inconsistency weaken the causation opinion as well as the expert's overall presentation.

The final section is the discussion or explanation section, in which the expert is at liberty to set forth in detail the reasoning relied upon for the opinions. The opportunity may now be taken to answer any remaining questions posed to the expert in the original assignment. Here, also, potential alternative causes can be discussed with explanation and justification offered for their rejection.

Hints and Suggestions

Attributes of a good report include faithful inclusion of all the statutory elements, as applicable (history, examinations, findings, test results, diagnoses, prognoses, and conclusions) as well as meeting all statutory time requirements.

The right balance between readability and technical details is to be achieved. Also required is conformity to and consistency with accepted professional standards and norms. In this connection, all clichés are to be avoided. While the expert's readership will naturally have a general understanding of the meaning of most figures of speech, they are by nature less precise and definitive than is desirable for formal written presentations. The expert should acquire the ability to describe any event, concept, or argument in economic, persuasive, and succinct prose. Similarly, imprecision and mushiness of thought and expression (not to mention vocabulary) are strictly to be avoided.

Certain vocabulary and word choices cause potential problems. Many such word choices fall into the category of inviting an attorney questioning an expert on the report to ask "gotcha"-type questions. Words that are often used to soften formal prose can cause problems. Such words and their adverbial counterparts include "typical/typically," "actual/actually," and many others. They potentially invite questions about what is not typical or not actual. Similarly, the "editorial we" (sometimes called the "imperial we") that is occasionally used to formalize and objectify writing, can invite snarky questions about who else was involved beyond the reporting expert.

Often there is a need felt to recast in simpler terms a preceding concept or argument that is complex. Many transition words used to lead into such recapitulations are trite. These transitions should routinely be accompanied by "in other words" or "to restate in simpler terms."

Imprecision is anathema to good report writing. Commonly utilized phrases like "in my experience," "it appears," "possibly," "in any event," and "likely" while thoroughly acceptable in most prose, inject imprecision into reports. Although they may be intended to add neutrality and dispassion, they actually detract significantly from the impact, decisiveness, and professionalism of the opinion. They dull rather than sharpen the focus of report writing.

To the greatest extent possible, avoid using ranges (e.g., "eight to twelve weeks of conservative treatment"). The range offered is almost never considered. Based upon interest, the one side hears and adheres to "eight weeks" and the other side, "twelve weeks."

The expert's report should stay independent and unaligned. The expert should write what is authentically thought in an objective and fair manner. There should never be any concern or impulse to shade the report and its conclusions or to please its recipient(s).

It is to be borne in mind that an unfavorable report is fully as valuable to its recipient as a favorable one. The unfavorable report is of great value in coming to terms with the realities of the case. Also, it assists in moving the matter toward resolution by settlement when that is appropriate. In this connection, many referring attorneys prefer for their expert to contact them before doing the report if it "looks bad." However, many do not. It is a wise policy for the expert to fully understand the referring attorney's preference on this matter from the beginning of the referral.

Adjectives and adverbs add color and dimension to writing generally. In reports, however, they can detract from the objective flavor of the report. Words of this kind add little if anything at all to the substance of the statements being made. Worse, they are often seen to betray prejudice or bias. Words such as "flagrantly," "blatantly," "unaccountably," "debatably," "obviously," "untruthfully," "unconvincingly," and "questionably" should be employed judiciously if at all.

Rote, fill-in-the-blanks, and formulaic reports or formats should never be used. Every report needs to be an original work. The most effective expert reports contain careful description of what the expert truly thinks in an unvarnished manner.

Since the report is directed to legal people most likely already involved in litigation, it is going directly into the adversarial arena of legal matters. The expert needs to have a fluent understanding of concepts such as "proximate/legal cause" and, for physicians, "exacerbation" as opposed to "aggravation." ("Aggravation" connotes a permanent worsening of a pre-existing condition. "Exacerbation" means a temporary worsening of the severity of a pre-existing condition which worsening subsequently resolves.)

Within the confines of statutory requirements, the report should not be rushed. Before promulgation, it should be set so it will not change unless upon significant future or additional development.

Finally, all experts (medical experts especially) should recognize that in doing expert witness work, they do not enjoy the automatic credibility that exists when a patient or client walks into their office for professional services. For example if hired by the defense in a case, the expert (and by extension the expert's report) is meant to persuade a skeptical plaintiff, plaintiff attorney, jury, and judge, none of whom are patient or client. Effective expert report writers are not lulled into any false sense of security that might otherwise result from the good favor and trust that they daily experience from their own clients and patients.

Before moving on to the matter of effectively preparing for and giving quality expert testimony, a detailed examination of the question of dealing with contention generated by opposing counsel in examinations and inspections is in order. Also offered will be some general discussion about what can be expected from opposing counsel in a litigated matter.

CHAPTER TEN

CONTENDING WITH CONTENTION

The most frequently expressed preoccupation at workshops and seminars on expert witness practice is disruption and interference with the investigation or examination of the expert, primarily by attorneys for the adverse party. In view of the adversarial nature of the development and progress of the Common Law, it is not a surprise that contention should often arise.

The spirit of the adversarial system is to find truth through the competition and contention between differing sides of issues and cases. It is to be expected that there will be significant contention at all stages of legal matters. Lawyers would not be complying with their professional and ethical obligations if they did not engage vigorously in the adversarial nature of the practice. In short, the contentiousness of law practice is expected, normal, and actually desirable. Those who engage in it are in a very real sense "just doing their jobs."

On a less high-minded level, it is undeniable that the contentiousness of law practice is fed by the fact that there is almost always significant money at stake. The law is actually somewhat limited in its ability to recompense wrongs and restore losses to legitimate victims. Essentially the only vehicle of compensation available to the law is money. Money can compensate but cannot always restore. While money can compensate, say, for a nasty scar, it cannot restore a client to the preaccident condition. Thus much of what is done in legal cases is to translate injuries into money values and secure payment or, conversely, to prevent or minimize such payment.

Following this line of reasoning, many people have or think they have valid claims. The challenge is to convert a claim into a verdict or judgment and thus into money into the claimant's bank account. To accomplish the conversion of a claim to money, a claimant will usually need an attorney. In that ever so prevalent eventuality, the claimant and attorney make common cause by entering into what is essentially a contractual partnership (the contingency fee agreement).

The claimant's attorney invests significant professional and financial resources in the partnership. Since, from the viewpoint of the defense, the goal of the expert process is ultimately to take money out of that partnership, it is typically fiercely resisted. Similarly, from the claimant's standpoint, the expert process is undertaken with the expressed purpose of maximizing the amount of money collected. It is thus a direct threat to the defendant's (and usually the defendant's insurance company's) financial interest. In these circumstances, when it occurs, notable contention can hardly be a surprise.

The adversarial nature of law practice notwithstanding, contention, as will be explained below, is remarkably much less frequent than is commonly feared by many experts. However, when it does occur, it can be greatly arresting for the expert participant, who, unlike the attorneys involved, does not deal with it regularly.

In this connection, some attorneys have observed the operation of the 85/14/1 Rule. Under it, approximately 85 percent of site views, vehicle inspections, and independent medical examination involve no contention at all. Of the remainder, some 14 percent may have some issue, but, by the end of the examination, an amicable resolution is achieved. Only about 1 percent or less of procedures ever involve any significant contention.

Dispute occasionally arises over the scope of the history that the examiner elicits. In the same way, experts are from time to time frustrated by the refusal of the examinee and attorney to comply with all elements of the expert's typical examination or investigation protocol. Quarreling may arise over issues of recording the examination by way of audio, video, or stenographic recording and, by extension, whether a reciprocal recording may be made. Some states specify the types of recordings that may be made, but many do not.

Strategies can be evolved to finesse objections to history taking or refusal to complete one element of the examination or another. Leaving an area of inquiry when there is objection and returning to it later often is effective. This is so especially if the return is done near the end of the examination and is all that remains to be finished. Frequently, some nonconfrontive discussion may persuade the examinee and representative to agree to proceed. Thus the parties fully conclude the examination with no threat or possibility to either of court involvement or return for further examination.

The allowable activities of an observing party, if permitted, are of interest. For the purposes of illustration, under the California procedure as to independent medical examinations, the observer may monitor but not participate. The observer may suspend the exam if it is felt the examiner is abusive or tries to do unauthorized tests or procedures. Correspondingly, the examiner may suspend the exam if the observer disrupts. Resumption occurs after court motion.[51]

Either side can "suspend" (note the word used in the statute) for perceived abuse, but it is mutually risky to do so. The California statute does not define "abuse" or "disruption" in any particular detail. It is, of course, assumed that both sides will contribute a high level of cooperation to complete the examination. "Disruption" and "abuse" will generally be determined in the discretion of the judge on a case-by-case basis. Monetary sanctions are almost always assessed against the loser. Discretionary rulings are largely not appealable.

A good tactic, if significant disruption is occurring, is to endeavor to complete the examination to the greatest extent feasible. After that consider

---

51   California Code of Civil Procedure, Section 2032.510.

suspending it. This ensures that as much as possible is completed in case the result of the court motion is unfavorable.

Bear in mind that if the examiner suspends, it will then fall to the retaining attorney to make a court motion for resumption. Such a motion may or may not be granted. Even if granted, it may require monetary sanctions to be paid to the aggrieved party.

Careful advance preparation, coordination, and briefing (usually not in writing) with the referring attorney as to all foreseeable disputes with the examinee and representative are advised.

If the expert is unable to negotiate a friendly resolution to issues of these kinds, the disruption that has resulted from noncooperation is by no means fatal to the expert's completion of the assignment. As has been repeatedly noted, the result of any case and its value is what an independent jury says it is at the end of a trial. Unreasonable disruptions, setting up of roadblocks, and frustration of the expert investigation are matters to which juries are very sensitive.

In cases of deliberate and excessive impediments, the expert should document carefully all that occurs in objective and dispassionate terms and then complete the investigation or examination as best as possible. The referring attorney will be thus well-equipped to put before the jury evidence of any shenanigans engaged in to frustrate the process. This will almost always redound to the perpetrating party's detriment. Juries are very acutely attuned to equality, equity and fair play. They will usually hold it against the party who impedes legitimate investigation and examination.

Contention and the engaging by attorneys in the typical tussling that is a natural outgrowth of the adversarial nature of the practice of law can often be intimidating to the uninitiated. This is demonstrated by the aforementioned high level of concern among experts that surfaces early and often at training and continuing education sessions relating to expert witness practice.

The expert's first line of defense is to appreciate, as we have detailed above, that contention is squarely within the nature of the practice of law. Whenever possible, it is well to consider that much of the aggressiveness coming from attorneys is likely to be largely posturing and is not to be taken personally. Attorneys are often satisfied once a strong demonstration of advocacy for their client has been made and will relent and retreat from disruptive positions if dealt with deftly. The proverb, "A soft answer turns away wrath," almost always proves to be true.

Occasionally, though, nothing works, and the choice is to either accept the restrictions placed on the expert's activities or seek the assistance of the court. Interest in seeking the intervention of the court will vary from attorney to attorney and jurisdiction to jurisdiction. When all else has failed, careful documentation of the disruptions that makes a clear record of them and that will facilitate their being brought before the judge or jury is the most effective antidote.

Chapters 12 to 15 below deal in detail with the subjects of depositions and trial testimony. Before addressing those topics in formal detail, the following chapter is presented in order to offer an overview of those subjects in the context of the need for experts to confine themselves to areas of inquiry that are strictly within their own fields of expertise and to be able to resist the temptation to be drawn onto unfamiliar ground.

CHAPTER ELEVEN

A TRIP TO THE ISLANDS:
WHAT WILL THE OPPOSING ATTORNEY TRY TO DO TO ME?

For those of a metaphorical turn of mind, a lawsuit might be likened to a tropical archipelago, the various personalities, players, and witnesses that litter the seascape resembling the isles and islets of the island group. Judge Island predominates, and Attorney Island is quite prominent. Others, like Plaintiff Island and Defendant Island, are of great interest, as are the varying Witness Islands. The islands, of course, are of greatly differing sizes, shapes, features, and temperaments. Moreover, in most trials, there will appear one or more Expert Islands that are of undeniable intrigue and influence.

Thus, a penetrating analysis of the case and, in particular, the interplay between expert witnesses and attorneys can be meaningfully (if perhaps a little whimsically) thought of as a "trip to the islands." The process evaluates the strengths and weaknesses of each island, develops preferences, and discerns the high and low points of each: the pretty places and the pedestrian.

It has been wisely said that one of the goals of the trial attorney in respect to expert witnesses is to get them off of Expert Island (where they are difficult to attack) and onto Attorney Island, where the terrain is more favorable. On Expert Island, the expert is confident of the lay of the land and knows intimately every geographical feature. But for the professional expert, Attorney Island has perilous and unmarked curves and dark back alleys that are fraught with danger.

The attorney's job is to entice, or if necessary drag involuntarily, experts onto Attorney Island, where the gravamen of their testimony can most effectively be called into question and impeached. The expert's strategy is to stay on Expert Island, which is home, where the culture is favorable, and which is the great repository of professional knowledge and experience.

The hallmarks of effective and persuasive expert testimony are credibility, consistency, and cogency. The attorney will attack these strong points and endeavor to reduce them one by one.

Credibility is built slowly and deliberately, like reputation. It is the result of the favorable proving out of the witness's whole presentation. It takes time to build and, like a good reputation, can be lost in a mere moment of stumbling.

Consistency is holistic. It needs to be internal in the witness's presentation, holding together factually and logically from start to finish. It also extends to and includes the expert's examination, records, and reports as well as pervious testimony by deposition or in trial in other cases, the expert's previous writings and publications, and the professional literature at large.

Cogency is the power of the testimony to convince, compel, and persuade by means of a clear, forcible presentation of facts, ideas, and arguments.

The purpose of litigation is to seek the truth and do justice, but litigation's context is, as we have heretofore emphasized, frankly and overtly adversarial. The overall goal of the opposing attorney is to see expert testimony founder on the rocks of cross-examination. What strategies will be employed to get the expert off of Expert Island, where there is safety, and onto Attorney Island, where there is unknown danger? Where do pitfalls lurk? What traps may be baited and set? How will the opposition endeavor to wreck the credibility of the medical expert's testimony, destroy its consistency, and muddle its cogency?

In rather blunt vernacular, the attempt will be made to ensure that the expert, especially in the case of a doctor, looks like a quack. No offense is intended here. Deposition and trial are a serious business, and their intensity should not be underestimated. In reliance on the reader's good sense of humor and irony, it is hoped that acronym QUACKERY may represent a useful mnemonic aid. (As an attorney of many years' experience I am aware of my profession's shortcomings. I imagine by now that I have heard all the lawyer jokes. I hope not to be unmindful that an acronym on the word "shyster," for example, could also readily and piquantly be developed!)

The opposing attorney's attack on the expert will likely have some or all of the following elements:

Question the accuracy of the Curriculum Vitae (CV).

Undermine the details of the personal and professional relationship with the referring attorney.

Attack assumptions and scientific methods.

Condemn earnings from legal work.

Knock the expert out of the mainstream of commonly accepted science and professional consensus.

Expose incompleteness in the examination, report, or records review.

Reveal inconsistencies in previous depositions, trial testimony, or articles and publications.

Yank the expert's chain just for good measure.

Much of the above is self-evident, but for the purposes of clarity and completeness, some additional comments follow:

1. **Question** the accuracy of the Curriculum Vitae.

   There is little that a lawyer loves more than to get the virtually free gift of catching experts "off the bag" as the result of exaggerations or inaccuracies in their curriculum vitae. It may be human nature to embellish these kinds of documents a little from time to time. However, before embarking on any form of legal work, the expert's CV should be updated and scoured for accuracy and completeness. The idea is to err on the side of caution and eliminate or understate any entry that is not absolutely certain. The consequences of tarnished reputation and embarrassment are far too high to risk any little gratuitous "boost" in a CV's claims.

2. **Undermine** the details of the personal and professional relationship with the referring attorney.

To the greatest extent possible, relations with the referring attorney should be at arm's length. Experts will come to know (and probably like) the attorneys who refer them cases. There will be temptations to share the typical business "perks" of golf tournaments, sporting events, dinners, and drinks (and even, perhaps, more lavish events like fishing or hunting expeditions). These are to be strictly avoided.

The opposing attorney expends virtually no effort and loses nothing by asking about how many golf games or martinis the expert has been treated to by the referring attorney. The expert, having taken advantage of them, risks loss of credibility, particularly in the eyes of jurors who may not be financially privileged to enjoy this kind of luxury. This risk is all out of proportion to any true bias that may have resulted. It is nonetheless absolutely real.

It is a fact of modern life that preoccupation with neutrality and objectivity has risen to near obsessive levels. I once invited a colleague to lunch who had recently been appointed to the bench and who is a career-long friend. Notwithstanding the fact that that the lunch was not at his invitation, he insisted that he pay for it so as to avoid any appearance at all of impropriety. This sensitivity is common and goes hand in hand with expert work.

3. **Attack** assumptions and scientific methods.

A favorite strategy of attorneys is to elicit all of the bases, both facts and assumptions, for each opinion of an expert and then develop ways to attack both. Assumptions are an area of particular vulnerability. As simple examples, a doctor may assume that the patient is telling the truth as to medical history or may assume that there were no intervening injuries between the subject accident and the examination. The doctor's opinions are based on those assumptions, and if they can be proved erroneous (frequently an easy task), those opinions are now discredited, perhaps along with the rest of the doctor's testimony.

In addition, it is wise to avoid making assumptions that are out of conformity with the standard literature or if a very cogent explanation for them is lacking.

4. **Condemn** earnings from legal work.

This will happen literally every time an expert gives sworn testimony. Even the feeblest of cross-examiners will touch on the question of how much money is earned annually from the referring attorney, from the insurance carrier client, and from expert work generally. Experts need to be prepared for this well in advance. Some dodge these questions by not having the details at their fingertips. This is usually ineffective, as the attorney has ways and means to keep digging and to prolong the process. And it runs the risk of reflecting badly on the expert.

The best strategy is to be fully prepared for this line of questioning and to deal with it in an altogether matter-of-fact and unemotional manner. Experts are likely to be asked to estimate the proportion of work that they do for plaintiffs/claimants versus defendants/respondents. It is often the case that a doctor, for example, will do more defense work. This is nothing to be ashamed of. It is most often the result of the fact that claimants already have in place an expert doctor in the person of their treating physician/specialist when they seek the assistance of the attorney. However, defendants are always forced to seek independent medical experts on the open market. This can be articulated succinctly as the reason for any imbalance in legal work.

As to earnings, censorious questions about them should be answered with the shortest and most direct response possible. Make no excuses or explanations. The truth is that the expert who is working for the opposing attorney is likely charging that attorney as much (or more). The referring attorney will bring that out in the trial. As long as the expert witness has not been defensive on the subject, the question of who-charges-what, although ubiquitous in trials, is likely to be a complete "wash" and not to figure in the outcome of the case at all.

5. **Knock** the expert out of the mainstream of commonly accepted science and professional consensus.

Some years ago, when asbestosis and mesothelioma litigation was getting started in earnest, there appeared on the expert scene an individual from outside the United States who held the position that smoking tobacco was actually healthy and therapeutic for asbestosis patients. This individual had strikingly good looks and impeccable qualifications, and, with his elegant accent and presentation, he was a notably good witness. Yet the utter outlandishness of his position undermined entirely the other superior aspects of his presentation as an expert witness.

Mainstream objectivity is the order of the day in expert work. There may be a temptation to be enamored with some plausible but outlying theory or study. This is to be avoided. There is much junk science extant these days. It is occasionally persuasive to a jury, but usually not. Expert issues are, for the most part, straightforward and commonplace (e.g., causation of injury and reasonable damages) such that there is ample opportunity for good expert work without resorting to any new, untried, or novel science.

6. **Expose** incompleteness in the examination, report, or records review.

The examination and report, including document and record review, must be complete and orderly in full accordance with all accepted standards of practice. Any and all omissions, whether large or small, will be discovered and exploited in deposition or at trial.

In anticipation of actual testimony, every effort will be made through the closest scrutiny of the examination and report to develop grounds to question their thoroughness and professionalism. As a result, every case must be treated from the first contact as if it will be tried. Clichés though they may be, no stone must be left unturned, every "i" must be dotted, and every "t" crossed.

Examinations must be in all respects complete. For elementary example, consider the question of shoulder pain in a personal injury claim. If the patient is complaining of symptoms with one shoulder, the independent medical examination doctor must not fail to thoroughly examine the other. The examiner must then document the examination of both shoulders with a complete and accurate report that evidences the completeness of the process.

7. **Reveal** inconsistencies in previous depositions, trial testimony, or articles and publications.

One needs only to observe the modern mania that surrounds the vetting of candidates for high political or judicial office to know that practically everything that a person has ever done, said, or written is subject to discovery and exposure. This is largely the result of the explosion of electronic media in recent years.

Before ever giving sworn testimony, experts should recall what they have previously written in professional articles and journals and review them for consistency with anticipated testimony, along with any previous sworn testimony given, whether by way of deposition or trial. As has been previously emphasized, litigation is sharply adversarial. Attorneys and litigants have the resources and incentive to locate and use any previous evidence or writing that is inconsistent with whatever may now be stated.

It is acknowledged that it is not a simple matter to keep track of all of what one has written and said. Nonetheless, practitioners should consider having at their fingertips some form of access to all publications and previous deposition transcripts. Transcripts of trial testimony are harder to get, as they are typically not made unless there is an appeal in the case, but it can never hurt to consider means and methods to secure access to them if needed.

8. **Yank** the expert's chain for good measure.

    Somewhat akin to the heckling and abuse a baseball pitcher might get from the opposing dugout, it occasionally occurs that the opposing attorney will deliberately attempt to annoy and frustrate an expert witness for the sake of intimidation and the obtaining of psychological advantage. It is rarely useful to respond or reciprocate. Judges and jurors have little patience with these antics, and they very quickly backfire to the detriment of the perpetrator. Responding dispassionately and meekly ("meek" in the connotation of long-suffering and of power under control, rather than submissive) is the order of the day.

Make no mistake: expert practice is no vacation to a tropical paradise. It is hoped, however, that the suggestions and illustrations outlined in this chapter will be easy to remember, helpful in placing the process in good perspective and in developing habits and practices that will minimize the uncertainty and trepidation that always accompanies the giving of formal testimony under oath.

A friend once commented as we stood by the side of a rugby field and as he prepared to go in to the game," You never want to go on the rugby field unless you are ready to play." So it is with the giving of testimony in law cases. We now will get ready to play in earnest and will turn to the details of giving a good deposition to be followed by consideration of giving excellent trial testimony.

CHAPTER TWELVE

ON THE PLAYING FIELD: HOW TO GIVE A GOOD DEPOSITION— GENERAL CONSIDERATIONS

We have heretofore likened expert practice to the building of a house. The first stage of successful expert witness practice is the laying of a solid and stable foundation through professional investigation and the writing of a comprehensive, coherent, and cogent report that forms the basis for further participation in the case.

The second stage is the giving of a credible deposition and equates to the framing of the structure. In the deposition phase, based upon the solid foundation previously laid, the expert offers deposition testimony that is organized and structured, suitable for the support of future work if necessary, including trial testimony.

In its broadest definition, the term "deposition" refers to any statement or affidavit made under oath. In connection with this chapter, we will consider the somewhat more narrow, but exceedingly common, process of a formal statement under oath administered and stenographically recorded by a licensed court reporter. The attorneys for the parties attend and participate in the deposition, which is conducted in a question-and-answer format.

The subject of good deposition testimony will be considered in terms of some general principles, positive suggestions for giving good testimony, discussion of typical attack lines by the opposing counsel, cross-examination techniques, and discussion of the differences between deposition and trial testimony.

Overall Perspective

A word on perspective is useful. The deposition is, obviously, out-of-court testimony. No jury is present. No verdict will be rendered immediately after the conclusion of the deposition. Nevertheless, it is undeniable that cases are often won and lost in deposition.

One adage holds that "You can't win your case in deposition, but you sure can lose it." The idea is that no matter how good a deposition a witness gives, that performance will need to be reproduced at trial in front of the jury. However, since a deposition is recorded stenographically (and often videographically), if the witness says the wrong thing or otherwise turns in a poor performance, the poor deposition will be repeated before the jury, so that damage done in a deposition is guaranteed to become damage done at trial. The implication under this view is that extra attention should be given to avoiding saying or doing the wrong thing.

This is not to minimize the positive effect that giving a superior deposition can have on the future of any case going forward. The positive effects of a good deposition performance are undeniable.

There follow some generally accepted suggestions for giving a good deposition and avoiding giving a poor one.

Tell the Truth

Above all, tell the truth. To do so is any witness's legal and moral obligation, bearing in mind that the expert witness is allowed to offer opinions, a privilege accorded to no other class of witness. There normally are conflicting expert opinions in any case. The opinion with the greater credibility is the opinion that will prevail before the jury.

Nothing must ever been done that might even remotely damage an expert's reputation for the highest level of honesty, integrity, and believability. In addition, consistently and faithfully telling the truth is the most effective method of avoiding being trapped in any inconsistency.

Answer Only the Question Asked

The deponent should answer only the question asked. Anyone testifying and especially an expert witness should be clear on the question asked and answer only that question. There is often a tendency for witnesses to answer the question they *think* they have been asked rather than the question that was actually asked. In addition, there is occasionally a temptation to answer the question the witness *wants* to answer rather than the one asked. It is to be ensured that the only answer is to the question asked.

Don't Volunteer and Don't Guess

Volunteering information is strictly to be avoided. Attorneys have various strategies for developing the questions they ask in deposition. One of those strategies is to design questions and follow-up questions based on answers just given. The more information that the deponent offers, the more fodder is supplied to the questioning attorney for additional questions. There is often a tendency to believe that if more information is offered, the questioner will be satisfied and move on. Although it may seem counterintuitive, the more information that is offered, the more questions are likely, and the greater the prolongation of the deposition. Keeping a deposition short is often more a product of the deponent saying less than more.

Guessing is strictly to be avoided. Sometimes experts feel compulsion to offer answers to all questions out of fear of seeming ignorant or uninformed if they do not. When it is true and not overdone, "I don't know" is a perfectly good answer. Guessing equals loss of credibility.

Counsel is typically entitled to intelligent estimates if the witness is able to give them. Expert witnesses should have an acute understanding of the difference between an estimate and a guess. Most attorneys offer some admonitions at the beginning of the deposition, and included among them usually is a request that the deponent not guess. It can be effective to recall to the attorney this admonition in circumstances wherein the expert is being pressed to offer an answer that would be a guess.

Avoid Arguing with the Questioner

There may occasionally be a temptation to interrupt or argue with the questioning attorney. This is strictly to be avoided. It is the referring attorney's responsibility to contend with the other attorneys. The witness should leave arguing to the retaining attorney. Witnesses who indulge in arguing give the impression that they are biased.

Strive for Precision of Language

Experts should be well spoken and articulate. They should avoid using slang and not indulge in argot or patois. Exaggeration diminishes credibility. Avoid phrasing responses in terms of absolutes on the one hand as well as using hedge words and terms on the other. Answers couched in terms of "always" and "never" give the impression that the expert is advocating for the client. Advocacy is the role of the client's attorney. Experts should be objective and neutral.

Succinctness is a virtue. Crisp, concise, and clear responses are desirable. Rambling, convoluted, and complex answers are difficult to follow and cause the hearer's attention to waver.

Use Humor with Extreme Caution

Humor must be handled very carefully. While pleasantness and affability are greatly to be desired and are essential, humor is risky and dangerous and is to be avoided. Often humor is successfully carried off through inflection of voice, facial expression, comic timing, and other values beyond the plain and spoken word. Deposition transcripts record only the words spoken. They are extraordinarily sterile. Even appropriate humor, which is very rare, often fails to come out as intended on the black and white of the transcript page. The attorneys may engage in some joking. It is best to smile politely and remain above it.

Take Your Time

Lawyers have their preferred cadences and rhythms. They work to get witnesses to conform to them. This is to be avoided. It is advisable to pause briefly before answering each question. This lets the testifier control the pace of questioning and gives the referring attorney the opportunity to place objections on the record. It also allows time to think about the answer.

No Advance Agreement

Some questioning attorneys try for an advance agreement at the start of the deposition, whereby it is requested that an expert agree to respond to questions with only one of three possible answers: "Yes," "No," or "I don't know." This agreement is to be rejected completely.

Waiver of Reading and Signing the Transcript

Counsel sometimes proposes that the expert waive reading and signing of the deposition transcript. Referring attorneys may differ in their positions as to the advisability of doing so. The expert should understand, however, that in virtually all jurisdictions, the deponent is afforded the opportunity to receive or have access to the transcript once it is produced and to review it and to make corrections. If this occasionally requested agreement is made, the expert will not have the opportunity to make such corrections as may be necessary, and embarrassment at trial could result.

How Lawyers Prepare for an Expert's Deposition

The primary objective of attorneys in taking expert depositions is to determine the full details of and then dissect the expert's opinions. The best practice is to explore opinions first and leave expert qualifications and other ancillary matters to the end of the deposition. Basic inquiries include:

1. Who engaged the expert?

2. What was the expert asked to do?

3. What was actually done?

4. What opinions and conclusions were reached and will be testified to at trial?

5. Was there investigation, testing, or analysis that the expert would have liked to have done but was not done?

In the event that the expert made a report, it is likely to be reviewed in detail. The following three areas of inquiry as to each opinion expressed in the report, or offered at the deposition if there is no report, can be expected:

1. What does the opinion mean in layman's terms?

2. What is the basis of the opinion?

3. Is this all that the expert intends to say at trial in the matter?

Follow-up questions and the seeking of further details usually cover such topics as:

1. What material in the file supports the expert's opinions?

2. Whether the expert relied on anything outside of the file in reaching the opinions?

3. Whether any exhibits or documentary evidence have been or will be prepared?

4. What assumptions were made in making any conclusions?

5. What information was supplied by retaining counsel?

6. Whether the expert is familiar with the other side's experts and has any opinion of their qualifications?

7. Whether there are any other areas pertaining to the matter not yet discussed that the expert has formed opinions on?

Often, but not always, it is after securing the expert's opinions and the bases for them that the inquiry will move on to education and possible bias. In any event, questions can be expected about education, experience, background, and training as they relate to the matter at hand.

Many attorneys faced with an expert of undeniable qualifications will de-emphasize interrogation directed specifically at education and experience and will explore issues such as:

1. Whether the expert's experience is personal and recent?

2. Whether the expert personally completed the investigation and study or referred it to assistants or specialists?

3. Whether opinions are based on personal investigation or on what the expert has read?

4. Whether the expert is relying on special training and personal experience or general education?

Often experts are asked to identify texts, treatises, and articles upon which they have relied. (Note that typically an expert may be cross-examined only on documents that have been considered and referred to, if not frankly relied upon.)

Subjects of how much the witness has charged and will charge for work in the matter and the expert's general volume of legal work are almost always covered. The more thorough attorneys continue in this vein inquiring as to the expert's history of testifying for one side or the other, such as plaintiff vs. defendant or prosecution vs. defense. Also covered may be the expert's history with the retaining firm and the retaining attorney, and the percentage of the expert's income from litigation.

Returning one final time to the question of additional work usually concludes depositions. Request is often made that the expert advise through counsel if any additional investigation, research, analysis or testing is done either to develop new opinions or supplement ones already held. It is usually added that failure to do so will lead to a request that anything additional be excluded at trial.

Let us now turn to more specific principles for the giving of a high-quality deposition that allow the expert deponent to successfully express professional opinions and to combat efforts by opposing counsel to disqualify and discredit that testimony.

CHAPTER THIRTEEN

ON THE PLAYING FIELD:
HOW TO GIVE A GOOD DEPOSITION—PRINCIPLES
OF GIVING GOOD DEPOSITION TESTIMONY

The giving of a good deposition starts with complete and thorough preparation. Once properly prepared, the competent expert deponent gives careful attention to prior writings and statements that could be raised in an endeavor to impeach the witness. In addition, care is taken to strictly confine investigation and the offering of opinions to the expert's specific field of expertise.

Proper Preparation Prevents Poor Performance

This old alliterative adumbration has perhaps no greater practical application than in expert witness practice. Examination and investigation, methodology, verification of calculations, research, study of documentation, and reliance on others are all legitimate elements in the development of expert opinions that will successfully resist vigorous cross-examination.

The thoroughness and detail of the expert's examination and investigation is directly proportional to the strength of the resulting opinions. If appropriate, visit the scene. Doctors obviously need to see the patient whenever practicable. When possible, tests and measurements should be confirmed by multiple processes. Experts should verify that the places, circumstances, and instrumentalities being examined have not changed since the events in the case occurred. In short, the well-prepared expert will be able to justify and corroborate all factual information that has been relied upon in forming opinions.

When documents are involved, they need to be identified and indexed and then thoroughly studied. The expert needs to have quick and easy access to all documents upon which opinions are based. Efforts to clarify uncertainties and illegible entries should be made and documented.

All elements of any applicable protocols should be completed. Shortcuts, no matter how much they may be justified by circumstances, need to be avoided. The opposition will identify them and they will render the expert vulnerable to successful impeachment. It goes without saying that testing, investigation, and measurements that were incompletely or not carefully done give rise to inferences of slovenliness, lack of professionalism, and possibly bias.

Photographic documentation of the expert's investigation is in most cases essential. Contrary to the established rule of thumb of "less is more," with photographs, more usually really is more. Careful organization and cataloging is critical, and pictures can be made more interesting by including tapes and other measuring devices when appropriate. Some experts like to have taken a few photos with themselves appearing in them to humanize the process. Experts who regularly document findings by photography need to have at least a rudimentary understanding of good photography and the principles of lighting and composition.

In the same vein, when other equipment is used, such as surveying, engineering, or electrical equipment, the expert must be proficient in its use, must have completely reliable equipment, and must be able to explain not only the use and purpose of such equipment, but also its manner of functioning.

Proven and accepted methodologies should be fully understood and faithfully followed. The opposition will likely retain an expert in the same field of expertise. The other side will know accepted norms, methods, and protocols. Whether in fact significant, any failure to comply with accepted methods will be questioned, with likely good effect. In addition, the expert needs to know and be proficient in explaining all methodologies, their rationales, and their purposes.

Often, such as in accident reconstruction matters or psychometric testing, arcane, esoteric, or otherwise complicated calculations are made and formulas used. The successful expert will verify these calculations and will be capable of performing them by hand or corroborating them independently. It should be anticipated that the expert, while under oath either at deposition or on the witness stand, will be asked to perform calculations, show the work, and explain the steps taken in reaching the results upon which the opinion is based. The ability to do this demonstrates care and thoroughness and catches potential mistakes before they cause public embarrassment.

Exhaustive research should undergird all opinions. Attorneys like to do research, and they consider themselves to be intelligent and precocious. Every expert needs to be significantly more grounded in research and better prepared than the questioning lawyer.

Attorneys, much more often than they should, frequently fail to provide to their experts all of the necessary documentation underlying the file. Experts need independently to verify that they have all relevant documents. These can include medical records, interrogatories, depositions, arbitration briefs, settlement demands, and documents produced by the parties pursuant to discovery. Once received all documentation should, of course, be read and carefully assimilated.

Most attorneys will agree that medical records consistently provide the greatest fodder for impeachment of opposition parties. One of my cases involved a young plaintiff who was injured in a rollover accident that resulted in his undergoing lumbar fusion surgery. He represented in deposition that he had had no previous lower back injuries, incidents, or medical treatment. The records of the plaintiff's primary treating physician were obtained. They consisted mostly of handwritten entries and were virtually illegible. This is not uncommon.

One entry, dated some three weeks before the accident, began with a single word that was very hard to read; it started with the letter "a." There were several more sentences that were utterly illegible. After returning to the entry numerous times and being frustrated by it, it was ultimately determined that the first word was "altercation." From there, it was determined that the young plaintiff had been in a barroom fight in which a bouncer had thrown him to the ground onto his back. His otherwise high value case unraveled from there.

It goes without saying, especially in cases involving medical experts, that all medical records should be obtained and reviewed.

Unique to experts is the privilege to rely on the work of others in forming opinions. Biomechanical experts regularly rely on the opinions developed by accident reconstructionists as to some of the essential details of what occurred and the forces exerted in the accident. Neuropsychologists similarly rely on other psychologists who conduct psychometric testing. If the information relied upon can be successfully attacked, then the expert's opinions based on it are suspect. Great care is to be exercised in choosing and relying on others. As with methodologies and calculations, the work of others needs to be independently verified and subject to convincing explanation by the expert who has relied upon them.

Be in Active Practice

The expert's credibility is greatly enhanced by active current practice in the profession, and inactivity, retirement, or emeritus status measurably detracts from it. The most successful medical experts are the ones who are currently practicing their specialty. Experts who take cases involving orthopedics or neurosurgery need to be actively doing surgery.

Many experts, especially physicians who are no longer doing surgery, object to this concept. They argue with considerable persuasion that the physician who is no longer doing surgery is relieved from the time pressures and economic constraints of active surgical practice and thus is free to devote the time and effort necessary to full and unbiased analysis of the matter at hand.

Nevertheless, the expert commenting on surgical matters who is not currently doing surgery will be challenged and impeached on this basis. It has become an unwritten requirement among many attorneys and insurance representatives that experts, all other qualifications aside, must be in the active practice of their professions.

The question is raised whether an expert should be doing expert work full time. This is not optimal, as it exposes experts to charges of bias in that their livelihood is arguably entirely dependent upon keeping clients happy.

Take Care with Prior Testimony, Articles, and Associations

In the modern era of the Internet and social media, it has become exponentially easier to access an expert's previous writings and testimony. Opposing counsel's task is to develop discrepancies, inconsistencies, and hypocrisy on the part of the expert. Exposing inconsistencies between the expert's testimony in the current case and prior statements or writings often does this successfully.

This situation is easily avoided. Experts should, as a matter of habit and practice, refrain from making pronouncements, giving presentations, or producing writings that are inflammatory, highly opinionated, or controversial. A high level of discretion should be exercised so as not to create any unnecessary history and record that can be raised against the expert.

Political, religious, sociological, or philosophical passion should be kept out of documentation that can be located and then attributed back to the expert. The essence of expert witness practice is objectivity and dispassion. Full commitment to expert practice obliges experts to set aside and defer participation in controversial activities while the expert is active in the practice.

Likewise membership in associations, clubs, and activities that are controversial or advance politically sensitive positions may be offensive to one group of jurors or another and should be avoided.

Stay on Expert Island

As has been discussed in detail in chapter 11, the wise expert assiduously remains on the comfortable ground of his own professional expertise and resists all requests to offer opinions beyond it. Experts must be diligent and consistently decline to be induced by referring counsel to undertake any assignment that exceeds their strict area of expertise. Similarly, competency in preventing opposing counsel from dragging them out of their area of professional comfort needs to be achieved by all expert witnesses.

Reciprocally, attorneys are well advised to stay on what might be thought of as Lawyer Island. Effective lawyers will refrain from attempting to give the impression that they know more than the expert about the expert's field. Wise attorneys resist the temptation to phrase questions in terms of "Isn't it true that ....?" Phrasing a question instead with words such as "Am I right that ...?" gives the impression that the attorney is well versed in the expert's subject but avoids an attitude of superiority. Experts can infer much about a questioning attorney based on clues offered by the manner and phrasing of questions.

Take Care in Criticizing Other Experts

More complex cases may have multiple parties on each side. It is every attorney's hope that opponents will be induced to begin fighting among themselves. This hope extends to opposition experts. Criticizing other experts should be avoided whenever possible.

Having reviewed general deposition considerations and the principles of giving successful deposition testimony, we now turn to the critical question of anticipating attorney tactics and also techniques that may be utilized in cross-examination.

CHAPTER FOURTEEN

ON THE PLAYING FIELD:
HOW TO GIVE A GOOD DEPOSITION—PREDICTABLE
ATTACK LINES AND CROSS-EXAMINATION TECHNIQUES

Experts' testimony ordinarily goes to both facts and opinions. But the essence of expert evidence is opinion. This reality leaves attorneys approaching the matter of cross-examination limited, for the most part, to exploration of the soundness and validity of the expert's opinions. Nonetheless, effort can be expected to demonstrate that the expert is unqualified, has utilized unacceptable methodology, is laboring under a conflict of interest, or is offering opinions that intrude into the jury's purview.

Quite often cross-examination will consist of fifty to sixty straightforward and guileless questions, with no attempt to trick, trap, or beguile the expert. Much that is significant may be omitted, whether intentionally or inadvertently. This happy circumstance is to be gratefully accepted with no attempt to assist or ensure completeness.

Or it may be that the greatest challenge that an expert faces is poorly or awkwardly phrased questions. Bad questions are very common and can be annoying to the expert. There often is an impulse, if not to lose patience, to assist by suggesting better phraseology to the interrogator. This is strictly to be resisted. The old political aphorism, to the effect that when your opposition is digging a hole, you should stand aside and let them keep digging, surely applies here. Even though the deposition may be tedious and prolonged, the inevitability of lousy questions should be expected and tolerated, and the flounderer left callously to his own devices and resulting fate.

Otherwise, there are a number of techniques, tactics, gambits, antics even, that attorneys employ from time to time in depositions of expert witnesses. The purpose is unnerving, intimidating, impeaching, and generally upsetting the witness. There is also the intention of lowering the expert's confidence and reducing credibility. Once recognized and understood, these tactics can be effectively addressed.

The Vulnerable Curriculum Vitae

Opposing counsel will carefully read and research the expert's curriculum vitae. The expert's CV should be scrutinized and brought up to date before any deposition.

Experts are strongly advised to have only one CV. There should not be different CVs that change from audience to audience.

Surprisingly, many CVs contain typographical and grammatical errors. These reflect poorly on the expert and should be eliminated.

Some experts include reference to past testimony and other unnecessary information. Past testimony and statements are a fertile field for the cross-examining attorney to develop lines of impeachment. Including information about this history in the CV makes the opposition's task easier. Similarly, there often is a temptation to include distracting and irrelevant information about the expert's unrelated associations and memberships. Political associations and positions, active participation in controversial associations and activities, and "vanity" activities should be left out.

Exaggerations and overstating achievements are absolutely deadly. Degrees earned, grade point averages, class standings, and other educational attainments must never be plumped. It is a simple matter for the opposition to verify these kinds of claims. The damage to an expert's credibility as the result of having been exposed for untruthful exaggeration is disastrous but completely avoidable by ensuring that the CV is accurate.

Conversely, oftentimes important credentials, licenses, or qualifications are omitted. All essential, relevant, and required credentials need to be included so as to avoid questions about their absence.

It is wise to cast CV entries in objective and understated terms. Truly well-qualified experts do not need to claim to be "world renown" or "nationally recognized" in their CVs.

Update Your Website

Experts should never neglect their websites. They need to be kept current, accurate, and consistent with the CV.

Assumptions, Factual Bases, and Presuppositions

After ensuring complete accurateness of the expert's CV and website, the next step in deposition preparation is the review and cataloging for accuracy and validity of all factual, logical, and professional assumptions.

Beyond attacking an expert's qualifications (or claimed qualifications), perhaps the favorite approach to impeaching an expert is to elicit and obtain clear commitment by the expert to all underlying assumptions, factual bases for opinions, and presuppositions. Then effort is made systematically to dismember them. The expert often will be reminded of one assumption or another and asked to confirm that opinions are based on it. Then will come the obvious request to acknowledge that if the assumption should turn out to be invalid or incorrect, it would follow that the opinion based on it must likewise be incorrect.

The line of argument now is easy. No matter how articulate or persuasive the expert's opinion may be, if the facts and assumptions underlying those opinions are invalid, then the opinions themselves are equally invalid.

Criminal History, Civil Judgments and Professional Discipline

Prior criminal convictions, such as for perjury or any other matter involving moral turpitude; large civil judgments for malpractice, fraud, or other dishonesty; or a record of professional discipline for serious violations of professional or ethical requirements are likely complete disqualifications for someone desiring to become a professional expert witness.

If there is a history of minor offenses or some other manageable controversy, referring counsel may be able to secure a favorable ruling from the court on a motion *in limine* precluding the opposition from mentioning the matter. Obviously strict transparency with and disclosure to the referring attorney is essential in keeping control of these kinds of issues.

In any event and however dealt with, the response to negative history needs to be confronted confidently, openly, and directly.

Fees and Charges

Contingency fee arrangements are to be strictly avoided. Some professions' ethical rules prohibit them and for good reason.[52] The fact that an expert has a financial stake in the outcome of the case is the most basic red flag for an attorney whose role is to question the expert's credibility. Chapter 20 is devoted to fees and charges, but for the purposes of deposition, the best position is to have been paid an hourly fee for all work and testimony time. Another advantage to be working by the hour is that there is no question, as there might be if a flat fee is being charged, of failing to take the time to do complete and top-drawer work.

---

52   See, e.g., American Academy of Orthopedic Surgeons, Code of Ethics for Orthopedic Surgeons, Section V.C.

Spread the Work Around

Many experts confine their work to a very limited number of clients or strictly to only one side. Just as it is unwise for experts working in the construction field to limit their work either to the homeowner side or to the development side, and just as it is unwise for physicians to limit themselves either to the plaintiff or the defense side, all experts are well-advised to divide their work as equally as possible between or among the primary competing camps.

Videotaping

Additional considerations are raised when the expert's deposition is videotaped. Video staging is susceptible to manipulation to the deponent's disadvantage. The videographer's setup and background deserve attention before the recording begins. Deponents should avoid any arrangement that makes it appear that they are looking away from the camera while testifying.

Occasionally, opposing counsel will engage in various sorts of antics designed to distract and to cause the deponent to appear less credible to the video camera. Questioning from a standing position, putting a leg up or one foot up on the conference table, walking around the deposition room, cracking knuckles, or fiddling with papers or other items will inevitably catch the attention of the expert deponent, cause the gaze to appear to wander, and possibly create the appearance of untrustworthiness. These antics are countered by mentioning for the record that they are occurring and requesting that counsel desist.

Typical Intimidation Techniques

There are several tactics that some counsel employ with the intention of intimidating expert witnesses, interrupting their concentration, and provoking anger. These are uniformly countered by advance awareness of them and by expecting them to occur so that they do not come as a surprise and cause frustration.

Caustic, cynical, or personal challenges to the witness's education, experience, or reputation are designed to annoy the expert and produce an intemperate reaction. This tactic is often accompanied by an arrogant and unfriendly manner. The witness may be subjected to a distant and cold demeanor or unfriendly glaring, not only during the deposition, but also before and after as well.

Sometimes counsel will accompany the foregoing at the outset of the formal deposition questioning with a snarly and contemptuous line of questioning designed to unsettle the witness from the very beginning. This may include an ominous line of questions confirming the witness's understanding of the gravity of the process and potential liability for perjury if answers are not in all respects true.

It is from time to time pointed out by questioning counsel that the deposition could be used against the deponent in some future proceeding. Conversely, an attempt may be made to lay a level of guilt at the feet of the expert by commenting that the testimony could be used to deny the questioning attorney's client medical treatment or some other type of benefit. Once in a while, the opposing attorney will have the client present for the expert's deposition. Strictly truthful answers are the correct responses to these moves.

Another off-putting technique is close and prickly interrogation as to the minutiae of the case. Dates, names, places, and all manner of other small details may be archly demanded. Thorough preparation covers, by memorization if necessary, these aspects of the file along with all others.

An attempt may be made to confound and confuse the expert deponent by asking compound or complex questions. Care needs to be taken to have such questions divided up. Otherwise, the response, although given only to one element of the question, may be made to appear as if it is made to the entirety. In that way, the answer inadvertently adopts unintended information.

Prolonged silences and staring are sometimes used in the hope that the witness will be flummoxed into continuing to speak when a question has already been fully answered. The hope is that the expert, in continuing to talk, will divulge information that is unfavorable or that can be effectively used for further questioning. A corollary tactic happens when the attorney acts unprepared and confused in hopes that the expert will try to help out by offering information that has not been elicited by appropriate questions.

Censorious questions about conversations that the expert has had with the retaining attorney can have an intimidating effect. It is wise to avoid speaking with retaining counsel during breaks so that this line of questioning and its implications of collusion can be avoided.

From time to time, if the deposition is done at a location other than the expert's own office, the deponent may be placed in less than optimal physical circumstances: a poor chair, uncomfortable temperature, or sunlight in the deponent's eyes. Objection should be immediately made and the conditions corrected. (Many experts prefer to have depositions taken at their own offices. Beware, however, that opposing attorneys frequently will agree, with the intention of having a look around the expert's office for books, publications, or other items that might provide material for effective cross-examination.)

A rather creative gambit that some attorneys are able to effectuate is that of constantly changing topics, leaving and returning to issues with no apparent order or purpose so as to promote confusion or inconsistency. The antidote for the expert is carefully taking the time needed to answer each question and maintaining strict concentration while avoiding the temptation to "psych out" or guess where the attorney is going.

Some attorneys will unduly and unjustifiably prolong the deposition. This produces fatigue and promotes mistakes. It also disturbs and worries the deponent as concern over other obligations may begin to intrude as the proceeding continues long beyond what was expected. Time limits for each session should be established before the deposition begins and strict adherence to them then demanded.

In a construction defect case several years ago, an experienced attorney subjected an equally experienced architect expert to this technique. The case involved condensation formation and rotting damage in the crawl space of a commercial building below a large refrigerator. A scientific document known as the psychromatic chart figured in the case. The psychromatic chart was used to predict condensation at various different temperatures and humidity levels. It looked like a piece of graph paper reflected in a psychedelic mirror. It was extraordinarily difficult to use, understand and interpret.

The attorney belabored the expert with questions about the chart for at least an hour and a half. The witness responded with patience and aplomb. When, ironically, the attorney himself finally started to become exasperated, the architect, with perfect timing, calmly stated, "You know, Attorney Jones, this is not rocket science."

The room erupted in appreciative laughter. The attorney was thoroughly chagrined. The subject of the chart *was* extremely complicated. If not quite rocket science it was close to it. The attorney had tried to wear down the architect expert, but instead of appearing foolish, the expert succeeded in flipping the attorney's tactics against him. With a quick verbal jab and to the delight of almost everyone present, the witness actually turned the tables and made the attorney look foolish.

It is very common at the end of the deposition to be asked a number of questions as to whether the expert has opinions not yet mentioned. Also, whether further work is anticipated that may generate additional opinions is usually covered. Care needs to be taken, in coordination with referring counsel, to give answers that provide future maneuvering room for the expert. Thus the expert avoids becoming limited in later testimony only to activities that have occurred up to the time of the deposition.

Relying on Hearsay

The general rule is that experts are allowed to rely on hearsay evidence. This gives experts significant latitude not afforded to other witnesses. However, there are limitations, and evidentiary rules require that hearsay evidence relied on by experts must be of the type "reasonably relied upon by experts in the particular field in forming opinions or inferences upon the subject."[53] An effort may be made to impugn an expert's opinion by showing that it has been based unreasonably on hearsay. Experts should only rely on credible and commonly accepted hearsay information.

The Document Dump

The expert's file is normally produced at or before the deposition. It is a routine question to inquire whether any documents have been removed from the file. From the time of first contact, superfluous documents should be kept out of the expert's file and in no circumstances should anything be removed by anybody once it is placed in the file.

Experts should avoid making notes on documents that, when produced, will provide ideas to opposing counsel for questions. Similarly, experts are well advised to refrain from taking notes at the deposition, as questions about them are likely, and the expert may be asked to surrender them.

Counsel may come to the deposition armed with documents additional to those contained in the expert's file. These may be complex and lengthy. The ploy is in the face of time constraints to gain answers that are rash and not well thought out. Any documents produced that the expert has not seen deserve all necessary time for review and formulation of a considered response. Care and the required time needs to be taken not to vouch for the contents or authenticity of documents that the expert has not fully vetted.

---

53   Federal Rules of Evidence 703.

Difficult and Tricky Questions

The matter of contending with difficult and tricky questions starts with careful listening. The expert deponent should listen to every word. Avoid rushing to begin an answer. The answer should not be started unless the question is completely understood. Judicious (but not too frequent) requests for clarification or repetition can be effective.

The graceful concession, when appropriate, often effectively manages a difficult question. Giving ground on minor points with grace and good cheer increases credibility. Attorneys have been known to fish for concessions, hoping that the expert will instinctively and curtly decline them and thus damage believability.

Likewise, an expert needs to admit any mistakes that may have been made. Mistakes are common, and jurors understand that they occasionally occur. Adamant denial of an obvious mistake promotes distaste among the jury. However, if a question contains a false assumption, manipulated factual premise or other mischaracterization, no concession should be made and the false premise should be challenged.

When hard questions are asked, directness often is a useful antidote. If asked a number or other datum that the expert does not know or cannot remember, a direct admission of the obvious avoids the appearance of evasiveness. It also leaves the questioning attorney with nowhere to go by further pursuing that particular line of questions. It promotes moving on to the next topic.

Conversely, when the expert is correct and declines to admit error in a given area as the questioning attorney hopes, often the approach is to start a line of questioning seeking to secure the expert's agreement with very broad principles. The attorney will then proceed to progressively narrow the questions until the expert is compelled to agree with a proposition that is contrary to the originally stated opinions. Defense against this begins with careful hearing of the broad questions and declining to agree entirely with the broad principles offered, unless it is possible to do so in every case.

Hypothetical questions are a favorite vehicle with many attorneys. They are discussed in detail in chapter 16. In brief, however, hypothetical questions will often assume different facts than the expert assumed when reaching the opinions stated. The hope is to secure assent to the new facts and so to turn the expert to agreement with the opposition's theory of the case. The essence of any hypothetical question is the facts requested to be assumed. These must be heard and understood completely. They need to be rejected if not entirely complete and accurate or if facts have been omitted.

If a difficult question requires an explanation, it is better to give the explanation first before responding "yes" or "no." Once the "yes" or "no" has been stated, counsel will usually attempt to stop any further response. Similarly, some experts believe that it is clever to respond to a question by saying, "Well, yes and no," and then proceed to add or subtract facts from the question. This constitutes the expert's own phrasing of the question and is not allowed.

One last tactic that is frequently encountered involves the attorney suddenly asking the expert to define some legal "term of art," securing an incorrect definition and then attacking the expert's opinion as based on fallacious understanding of applicable legal terms. Such terms as "probable cause," "legal cause," "aggravation," "exacerbation," "medical certainty," "medical probability," "standard of care," and "open and obvious" are all terms that are heavily freighted with specialized meaning. Experts need to have a complete and comfortable working knowledge of them.

Along with having the reputation for writing a great report, one of the best recommendations that can be made about experts is that they give an excellent deposition. The process, as has been seen, can be complicated and intricate. There usually is a learning curve that an expert goes through to perfect the giving of credible and persuasive depositions. Once that curve had been negotiated, the ability to succeed in deposition is an asset of immense importance for the quality expert.

Without any doubt, the giving of an excellent deposition has the potential of measurably advancing the possibility of favorable settlement of the case. Otherwise, it forms the strong and stable framework for the expert's trial testimony in the event that the case is not settled.

Excellent report writing and superior witness ability in deposition often do lead to settlement; occasionally, however, these attributes do not produce that outcome. It is now left to consider the eventuality that it becomes necessary to prepare for and attend trial.

CHAPTER FIFTEEN

THE BIG SHOW: SUCCEEDING AT TRIAL—A SUCCESSFUL DIRECT EXAMINATION

If the expert's investigation and report are the foundation upon which all following work on the case is laid, and if the expert's deposition is the structural framing upon which the remainder of participation in the matter is hung, then the expert's trial testimony is the finish work with all its livability, utility, and visual attractiveness.

Exceptional trial testimony differs significantly from deposition testimony and needs to be understood in terms both of good direct testimony (this chapter) and effective resistance to cross-examination (chapter 16).

Contrasting Deposition and Trial Testimony

Many experts who have significant experience in both deposition and trial testimony treat the two situations very distinctly. In deposition, veteran experts will often engage the opposing attorney with a profusion of technical "inside baseball" colloquy. It is replete with technical terms and concepts highly specific to the expert's field and is difficult for the attorney to interact with. This tactic takes up time, makes follow-up questions difficult, and distracts some attorneys from their cross-examination plan. Concededly frustrating from the standpoint of the attorney, this is a good example of staying on Expert Island.

At trial, however, under direct examination, the expert applies all teaching and didactic talent to explaining the opinions to the jury in understandable, manageable terms that can readily be assimilated by the uninitiated.

For their parts, attorneys also usually utilize different approaches with experts at deposition and at trial. Most attorneys recognize that the primary purpose of the deposition is investigatory, but that there is also a significant secondary forensic component. The first goal is to get the facts of the expert's opinions listed, fleshed out, and set in stone. Then, whenever possible, there is a secondary purpose: to secure statements that can be used against the witness later in the proceedings, especially at trial.

The competent attorney uses the expert deposition as a matter of first importance to secure full development of the expert's facts and opinions, even if they are unfavorable. Some attorneys mistakenly view expert depositions as if they were trial testimony. They avoid questions that could elicit testimony unfavorable to their client's interest. Such attorneys often will rejoice, for example, when a colleague elicits information in a deposition that is damaging, but this is a shortsighted view.

The most effective attorneys use the deposition to get out all the facts, pin those facts down, and obtain assurances that they have the whole of the expert's evidence. Then in the interim, between the deposition and trial, the expert's opinions can be carefully examined and successful attacks on those opinions developed for the time of trial. The goal is to elicit testimony from the expert that can be used on cross-examination for impeachment at trial.

In order to ensure the completeness of aggregating the expert's facts and opinions, many good attorneys display friendliness during deposition. Some will act, as has been mentioned in chapter 14, uninformed and hope that the expert's desire to be helpful will result in significant volunteering. Many use an open and friendly approach. Drama and the "kill shot" are saved for trial. Usually attorneys will ask at trial only questions to which they already know the answer. The deposition context is freer, the attorney can explore, and there is the opportunity to become familiar with and understand the expert's personality.

Cross-examination at trial is intended to elicit specific and definite points. Questions are much more tightly phrased. The answers sought are shorter and more specific.

Excelling in Direct Examination

As with deposition testimony, the value of complete and proper advance study and preparation by the expert cannot be overemphasized. After uncompromising preparation, the elements of an excellent direct examination are confidence, the ability to teach, organization, and skill in communication.

Study and Preparation

Little guarantees persuasiveness, confidence, and self-assurance like thorough preparation. At trial there are many vicissitudes that are beyond the expert's control, such as what questions will be asked. Preparation, of course, is not beyond the expert's control but is entirely and exclusively up to the expert. Experts must never stint on preparation.

A certain level of advance planning for direct examination between the expert and the retaining attorney can be valuable. In fact, settling in advance on several matters is vital. These include efficiently and effectively presenting to the jury the expert's qualifications in an engaging and complete but not overbearing manner (that is, without either boring or boasting). These matters also include settling on the level of detail desired from the expert in response to referring counsel's direct examination questions. Finally, the expert and attorney should cover the use of carefully crafted questions in eliciting the expert's opinions that will captivate the jurors' interest and segue smoothly into the details of the opinion.

It is surprisingly common for attorneys to rush through the portion of expert direct examination in which the expert's qualifications are offered. Hurrying through this portion of direct examination can be a mistake and it threatens the loss of significant advantage before the jury. The qualifications phase of direct examination represents a golden opportunity for the expert to connect with the jury. Connection to the community, associations, employment history, and military service, if any, are all legitimate elements of the expert's qualifications. When presented to the jury, these data offer the possibility of fostering bonds of affect and sympathy between the jurors and the expert.

The pathway that the expert has traveled to arrive on the witness stand is almost always of interest to the jury. It can create sympathy for and appreciation of the expert by the jury. Reasonable, selective, and not boring details of the expert's educational career, internships, residencies should be brought out. Moreover, offering the details of work on scientific studies, and participation in the development of scientific and medical devices and testing equipment provides to the jury a very personal and compelling view into what it has taken for the expert to reach professional prominence.

The expert should be introduced and defined by the direct examination and not by cross-examination. The relationship of the expert's specific qualifications to the issues being presented to the jury can and should be emphasized at the outset.

Proceeding then to substantive evidence, the expert should develop with counsel strategies for ensuring that counsel's questions afford the expert the opportunity to show the extent to which opinions are objective and factually based. The questions should also elicit good illustrations (including the use of audiovisual aids), metaphors, examples, and analogies. It can be mutually agreed to avoid insider language that is not easily understood by the jury.

Effective coordination before the direct examination has the added benefit of avoiding awkward situations that otherwise often occur in front of the jury. If the retaining attorney feels that sufficient details have not been offered in response to questions, there may be inelegant requests to the expert to offer further details or explanations. On the other hand, if the attorney feels the expert is expounding excessively or is boring the jury, there may be uncomfortable efforts to interrupt the expert and suggest that a new topic be discussed. Good pretrial coordination will avoid these kinds of situations.

Questions can be planned that allow the expert to showcase the investigation, research, testing, and other efforts that have gone into reaching the opinions. Opinions alone, and without the context of the underlying factual and investigatory framework, are of less value and impact.

Confidence

If there is any one quality that sets the superior expert witness apart, it is confidence. Confidence results from an admixture of learning, advance preparation, and experience. It is expressed in secure, direct, and dispassionate presentations that are affable, open, and nondefensive. The confident expert is so grounded in thorough preparation, underlying study and education, and practical experience that a palpable, steady, and friendly directness results. The confident expert believes implicitly in the opinions offered, and this is reflected in affect and demeanor.

Ability to Teach

Since experts are allowed to offer opinions, much of what they are called upon to do before the jury is to teach. Adopting the attributes of a good teacher is critical. The presentation must be concise and pithy. It needs to be confined strictly to information that the jury needs in the particular circumstances of the case. Any tendency to demonstrate the full measure of the expert's knowledge of the field of expertise is to be avoided. The presentation should also be cogent, which is to say clear, coherent, and persuasive. Extraneous and irrelevant material should be eliminated.

Not only is brevity the soul of wit, it is also the essence of a quality jury presentation.

Concrete Components of Good Teaching

The matter of good teaching is not only a very large subject; it is also a controversial one as well. There is insufficient room here to unpack it in dispositive detail. There are, however, at least four concrete components to a good jury teaching performance: connecting, conversing, conveying, and convincing.

Connecting

Little connects with a jury like passion. Good teachers have an infectious passion for their subject. Passion leads to a presentation that imprints on the hearers' memories and captivates their attention and interest. It also evidences genuine character and integrity, which are the essence of credibility.

On a more prosaic level, good teachers are acutely aware of the jury's reactions and responses to their presentation. They can see whether the jury is understanding or is confused. Are they alert and responsive, or are some stifling yawns, nodding off, or even worse, falling asleep? Does their affect suggest engagement or indifference? The good teaching expert continually appraises all of these reactions while on the stand and can make appropriate adjustments on the move.

Connection is promoted further by being solicitous of the jurors, ensuring that they can hear and see and generally by treating them deferentially and respectfully. It is often possible to determine which among the jurors are the likely leaders, and a measured and balanced extra level of focus and attention can be given to them.

An anecdote illustrating how *not* to connect effectively is instructive. In a warehouse accident case, a human factors expert sought to muddy the waters by attempting to bury the attorney questioning him with a profusion of technical jargon, references to little known scientific principles, scientific literature that was virtually unread by anyone but him and general arrogance. At the end of a long and tedious answer, the expert suggested snidely that the attorney "could look it up." The questioner, with admittedly somewhat faux amiability, then asked, "Why would you think I need to look it up?" In truth he had no idea what the expert was talking about, but neither did anyone else. The bully's bluff was called and the expert's sympathy and effectiveness with his hearers were demolished.

Good eye contact and other positive body language are helpful in connecting, as in any other context. A pleasant countenance, leaning forward and toward the jury, smiling and nodding, as well as avoiding harsher gestures like finger pointing, will all have good effect.

Conversing

A jury presentation is, of course, not a conversation in the traditional sense that both participants are allowed to speak. But it may be thought of as a conversation on a subtler level.

An effective expert witness takes the opportunity to demonstrate from models, charts, and other learning devices; expert teachers often move around the courtroom as the judge may permit, responding to the questions and the learning processes that the jurors are going though mentally without actually hearing them speak. It is possible by observing the jurors carefully to gather valuable input from them as to what they are thinking and how they are reacting to the presentation.

One seat belt expert effectively demonstrated and conversed by acting out his point. The case involved a plaintiff who hit his head on the rearview mirror when his car sideswiped a bridge railing. The defense was confident that plaintiff had not been wearing his seat belt. Otherwise, he would have been held in place and his head kept well away from the rearview mirror.

At the critical moment of his testimony, the plaintiff's seat belt expert mimicked loudly what it would have sounded like inside the car when contact was made with the bridge. He said, "Bam, bam, bam, bam, bam," and punctuated the words with syncopated knocking on the table. Then he pantomimed the plaintiff driver reflexively moving to his right, away from the noise and collision. He thus made a convincing point that the frightened plaintiff had stretched the seat belt up and away from the impact before its mechanism had a chance to lock. It was effectively shown that plaintiff could plausibly have both had the seat belt on and hit his head on the rearview mirror.

The artful use of language promotes a good conversation with the jury. Jurors come to their service with varying levels of formal education. Experts usually interact professionally in rarified academic circles, where professional argot and nomenclature are the norm of communication. Opinions and concepts are often said to need to be expressed at trial in language and terms that would be easily assimilated by an eighth grader. All experts must develop the ability to express the intricacies of their opinions and explanations in precise and universally understandable language.

Conveying

After connecting with the jurors and setting up the atmosphere of conversation, the next challenge is to effectively convey the salient points of the expert's investigation and opinions in a compelling, easily assimilated, and memorable way. As the minutiae of many professions are likely to be stultifying to the average lay juror, effort needs to be exerted to make the confusing clear and the boring exciting.

Many experts tend to make their points by setting forth their facts and reasons and then drawing their conclusions. Although it seems counterintuitive, the opposite approach seems to function better. Making the point first and then explaining it is easier to follow and remember. This method also tends to tie the expert's conclusion better to the facts and themes of the case. It also lets the expert get to the important matters first and foremost, in keeping with the principle of primacy, which is discussed in detail below.

Audiovisual is de rigueur in the modern era. PowerPoint, slides, analogies, charts, models, maps, and the like must be mastered and liberally used. Audiovisual aids also provide to the expert occasional opportunities to leave the witness stand to make demonstrations. This relieves potential monotony, increases interest and attention, adds animation, and promotes greater connection between the expert and the members of the jury.

Several years ago, even before technology was as advanced as it is now, a case was tried that involved an airplane crash into a mountainside in Alaska. One of the defendants was the publisher of the charts that the pilots were using at the time of the crash. Experts in several fields collaborated in creating a very effective audio-visual reconstruction of the minutes leading up to the disaster.

The presentation had three components that were all precisely coordinated. It showed both the plane's progress over the ground on a flat map and along a cross-section diagram that depicted the plane in relationship to the changing ground elevations over which it was passing. Added to all this was a coordinated recording of the pilots' communications with air traffic control.

Of course the presentation and especially the voice communications ended dramatically when the plane flew into high ground that was allegedly not adequately referenced in the defendant's charts. The plaintiffs' contentions concerning the claimed insufficiency of the defendant's charts were thus most effectively conveyed to the jury.

In conveying well, brevity is also foundational to good teaching. The good teacher expert will give time and thought to determine in advance what the jurors need to know and will resist the temptation to demonstrate erudition by offering more than is necessary.

Convincing

Some finer details of presentation assist greatly in convincing the jury of the thoroughness of investigation and correctness of conclusions. Giving attribution and recognizing sources of information ground the expert's presentation in the professional context and framework. It lends great credibility.

Citations of standard reference works and peer-reviewed studies confirm that the expert has been diligent in preparation and is not inventing anything. In addition, the testimony can be structured to allow the jury to follow the same road that the expert followed in getting to the opinions and conclusions.

It is possible subtly to emphasize important points with such phrases as "This is key" or "Here is a huge point."

An expert presentation that incorporated all of connecting, conversing, conveying, and convincing occurred in a vehicular accident case. The plaintiff was severely injured when she pulled out of a stop sign in front of the defendant, who was proceeding on a wide arterial street. Plaintiff contended that the defendant was speeding, and there were competing accident reconstruction experts.

The plaintiff actually had a team of two experts, who were very serious men. They had stiff, military bearing. They had buzz haircuts, wore dark suits and conservative ties, and were very buttoned down and clinical. One would testify and the other would track the points being made with a PowerPoint on a screen in front of the jury. The PowerPoint became the focus of their testimony. There was a lot of glitz in their presentation, but little compassion.

The defendant expert was an unusually pleasant and merry PhD. He was originally from India and appeared for trial appropriately but somewhat "tweedily" attired. He had a certain lilt to his voice and speech that was agreeable. When he took the stand, he brought out a hand-made matrix to illustrate his opinions as to why the defendant was not speeding. He explained his matrix in understandable and compelling terms. His passion for his subject and his opinions were infectious. He concentrated on the jury, and although he used his matrix effectively. The expert, rather than his matrix, was the centerpiece of his evidence.

It was a treat to watch the jury react to these different styles. They were edgy and tense, almost grudging as they watched and listened to the high-tech PowerPoint. But when defendant's expert took the stand, they visibly relaxed. As a group their countenances softened. There was a palpable breath of fresh air in the courtroom, and they lapped up the PhD's case.

Every element of a superior direct examination was present. Not only did the PhD's traditional presentation match the techno one, it conquered it. The verdict, of course, was for the defendant.

Organization and Skill in Communicating

If, as is usual, there is a deposition, it must be reviewed in detail and remembered thoroughly. The same is required as to any report that was submitted. The expert's file should be organized in advance so that quick and efficient access to any portion of it can be immediately had while the expert is on the stand, with no fumbling, shuffling of paper, or other waste of time.

Recent political debates have demonstrated that stating the main opinion or conclusion first, followed by the use of numbered lists, can increase persuasion: "My policy is correct on the basis of three points." "My opponent's plan is wrong for five separate and distinct reasons." It has been said that when an audience is given a numbered list of points to expect, they feel obligated to listen all the way through the numbers.

Numbered lists promote good organization and provide structure and relief for listeners of long tracts of information. This is not only seen in the law. Borrowing from another communication genre, it is a feature of good homiletics that a sermon is most effective with three to five clearly articulated and developed points.

The story circulates that a dynamic preacher was asked the secret of his success. He responded that there were three elements (the list). "First, I tell them what I'm going to tell them (the opinion/conclusion). Next, I tell them what I have to tell them (the underlying facts and arguments). Finally, I tell them what I told them (the summary)."

The principles of primacy and recency apply to expert testimony. The jury is likely to remember best both the first elements (primacy) and the last elements (recency) of the expert's evidence. It is desirable to start the expert's evidence with a compelling high point and similarly to save a second high point for the finish. Slavish adherence to chronological or some other order that is perceived as logical can give testimony the flavor of being canned and rehearsed.

The principle of primacy also dictates, in accordance with comments made above, that throughout testimony, the expert should follow the general order of offering opinions and conclusions first, with detailed explanations and justification to follow. Thus interest is more effectively captivated and opinions rendered more memorable.

Primacy and recency promote interest and increase retention. Every effort should be made to avoid boring the jury. Keeping answers short helps. Lengthy narrative answers quickly bog the jury down and promote mind wanderings and loss of attention. Good teaching is never boring.

Word choice dramatically raises the quality of communication. Direct language, vivid construction, and impactful phrasemaking are desirable when not overdone. Euphemisms, limp language, and formulations that evince mushy thinking are to be avoided. One attorney representing the plaintiff in an auto accident that had occurred on Christmas morning called the incident, to good effect, "the Christmas Crash."

As rudimentary examples, "died" is often better than "passed away," as is "aborted" rather than "miscarried." On the other hand, it is often preferable to use simpler and pithier vocabulary over longer and stuffier words, such as "he saw" rather than "he observed" or "she wrote down" rather than "she documented."

Likewise, linguistic precision is a great virtue. Fuzzy, squishy, or equivocal words and phrases (not to mention thinking!) diminish the forcefulness and impact of the expert's presentation. The word "apparently" as well as the phrase "to the best of my knowledge" are much overused and blur the definitiveness of the statements of their speakers. Precision and directness of speech exude confidence and competence. As their antecedents often are unclear, pronouns are frequently an impediment to clear statements. It is often worth the trouble to simply restate the person or thing to which pronouns refer.

Insiders regularly utilize abbreviations, verbal shorthand, and acronyms, but their meaning is often lost on the jury. The cognoscenti on a medical case will all likely know what "p.r.n."[54] or "q.v."[55] means, but lay jurors usually do not.

It is useful for experts to be aware that lawyers are taught to develop a theme for their case and to weave it throughout the various elements of their presentations. In one case the defendant was falsely accused of battery in conjunction with a barroom fight. The defendant had been subjected to numerous indignities as a result of his mistaken involvement in the matter, including arrest, criminal investigation with no charges ultimately preferred, and finally the subject civil trial. The theme chosen was "Enough is Enough." Sympathy was successfully generated for the defendant, and fortuitously, the day that the verdict was rendered was his birthday. Somehow the jurors were aware of his birthday and not only found in his favor but also all gathered around him after they were dismissed and congratulated him on his special day.

Experts and attorneys can work together to conform the expert's direct presentation to the overall theme of the case that has been chosen.

Finally, cadence and pace are important. Without doubt the most

---

54   Abbreviation for L. *pro re nata*, "according as circumstances may require": *Dorland's Illustrated Medical Dictionary,* 25th Ed. (1974), 1256.

55   Abbreviation for L. *quantum vis*, "as much as you please": ibid., p. 1300.

frequent complaint that certified court reporters make is that people "talk too fast." The stress and excitement of trial often cause both attorneys and expert witnesses to speak quickly. Good points get easily lost in torrents of rapid sentences. Just as bad is a lugubrious and drawn out style that causes the jury fervently to wish that the speaker would just hurry up and finish. A good cadence balance can easily be developed, which promotes attention and retention.

In the end, it is true that making a good jury presentation requires the accomplished expert witness to do some multitasking. There is the need to compose clear and precise answers while at the same time monitoring and assessing their effectiveness and the hearers' receptiveness. It may be considered a somewhat daunting task, but with practice it is readily attainable.

All of the foregoing suggestions for clear, concise, and coherent communication have as their goal to make the expert's direct testimony *memorable*. During the deliberations, the jurors are left for the most part with little more than their memories to guide them in deciding the case. The more that an expert can do to make direct testimony easy to remember, the better overall job the expert will have done for the client.

Now let us address the question of successfully handling cross-examination at trial and thereby avoiding the circumstance of having a quality presentation on direct examination demolished before our eyes.

CHAPTER SIXTEEN

THE BIG SHOW:
SUCCEEDING AT TRIAL—WINNING ON CROSS

Cross-examination on the witness stand by the opposing attorney(s) in front of the jury is the final scene in the last act of the drama that is the role of the expert in a litigation matter. Of course, not every expert referral will go all the way to trial testimony. While on average only a very small percentage of cases actually go to jury trial, virtually all of those cases have expert involvement. The likelihood that an expert in active practice will ultimately testify and undergo cross-examination is moderately high, and almost all trials will include the testimony of one or more experts.

From the lawyer's standpoint, the secret to successful cross-examination of any witness is to know whether to cross-examine and, if so, for how long and then when to stop. Once the decision is made to proceed, the tactics, strategies, and techniques used by attorneys at trial on cross-examination of experts fall under the same general rubrics as have been seen with respect to depositions. However, the context is different. By the time of trial, the attorneys have fully investigated the expert evidence in the case and are (or should be) thoroughly aware of the experts' investigations and opinions.

There is always the hope in cross-examining an expert that corruption, bias, incompetence, or untruthfulness might be shown. However, "Perry Mason moments," in which the witness breaks down and confesses his sins to the interrogating attorney, are extraordinarily rare. On a more practical level, the cross-examiner is far more likely merely to have success in garnering from the expert scientific facts that will help the cross examiner's own case rather than the case of the proponent of the expert.

Cross-examination questions are, for the most part, crafted in advance. Attorneys generally know the answers to the questions that they ask. From the standpoint of the cross-examiner, the best responses are "Yes," "No," and "I don't know." (Some attorneys, as has been detailed previously, develop the practice of seeking a deal [a deal to be rejected] with the witness that answers will be only those responses.) If the attorney can get these few short answers consistently, the cross-examination in practical effect allows the attorney to testify through the witness. Above all, the attorney should avoid posing broad and open-ended questions on cross-examination, as these types of questions afford the expert opportunity to expand and expound and perhaps even get into evidence information that the retaining attorney had failed to elicit.

Experts should anticipate that the cross-examining attorney will endeavor to follow the principles of primacy and recency and will generally try both to start and to end all cross-examinations strongly.

Attacking Assumptions and Investigation

The expert's personal efforts in investigating and developing facts will be closely examined. Attempts may be made to show that the expert merely accepted at face value selected, incomplete, or erroneous underlying facts from referring counsel. Similarly, counsel will endeavor to show that testing done was inadequate to support the expert's conclusions and opinions or that the expert lacks personal first-hand knowledge of the facts. Effort should be anticipated to demonstrate that the expert failed to include and rely on supposedly critical information unfavorable to the expert's client's interest. Finally, in addition to the details of the actual investigation, the expert's assumptions will doubtless be questioned.

Winning responses include the expert being able to testify to as much personal, hands-on investigation and testing as possible. The expert should be prepared to persuasively verify the accuracy and believability of all information provided by referring counsel. If any testing was not performed, justification for not having done so needs to be clear and convincing. This is particularly important to get across to the jury when the reasons are that evidence would have been destroyed by testing, or the testing would have been prohibitively expensive in relation to the magnitude of the case.

The validity of all assumptions must be carefully and completely confirmed. To the extent that there is an inference that an opinion is wrong if its underlying assumptions are fallacious, the expert's staunch defense of assumptions as true, accurate, and reliable undergirds them remarkably. The attack on assumptions is to be both anticipated and welcomed. When successfully refuted, the attack essentially backfires, resulting in notable confirmation of the expert's testimony.

First-hand knowledge is always the most persuasive. If it was not accessible, a creative, cogent, and coherent explanation needs to be made as to why it was not necessary and as to why it would not have changed the expert's conclusions.

Alleged Bias

Fees, patterns of previous work, suggestion of bias, or interest in the outcome of the case almost always come up on cross-examination. Many attorneys like to take the expert's hourly fee amount and either multiply it into an astronomical figure of monthly or yearly earnings or, conversely, divide it down to a scandalously high dollar figure per minute. The intended implication is that for such lavish sums, the expert would say anything the client wanted.

An experienced expert can expect to be cast on cross-examination as always testifying for only one side or as being a professional witness. As has been indicated, this approach is best defeated long before any trial occurs by the expert having diligently worked for both plaintiff and defense sides. It can be valuable to have readily at hand names and specific information as to clients the expert has worked for on the opposite side.

Often it is not practicable to have a strictly even-handed practice. There can be good reasons for this. In the medical field, plaintiffs often use their own treating physicians as experts. The field of independent medical examining is dominated by the defense, since claimant attorneys very frequently inherit their expert physicians from their clients. The expert should have ready plausible and persuasive explanations for any imbalances of this kind.

All attacks based on alleged bias need to be confronted directly and forthrightly. Obfuscation, sheepishness, or evasions are deadly. Jurors are usually sophisticated enough to know that experts are learned professionals and both expect and deserve to be paid for their work. They also understand that both sides are paying their experts. Straight, open, and nondefensive answers to these lines of attack are most effective. When thus handled, money issues and professional witness attacks usually are not seen as significant by juries.

Further insulation from charges of bias results from care exercised in avoiding undertaking matters and being involved in organizations and causes that can result in successful claims of lack of objectivity and neutrality, as has earlier been mentioned.

Direct Attack on the Expert's Opinions

Common attacks on the specific opinions that the expert has formed include suggestions of other potential causes, impeachment with prior inconsistent statements, use of damaging documentation, questioning the time of formation of the opinion, pointing out exaggeration, questioning disclaimers, and quibbling over the definition of certain terms and vocabulary.

Alternative causes or theories of causation may be suggested as sufficient to explain the incident. Time, effort, and imagination should be invested in anticipating these alternatives before the expert takes the stand. Thus, readily understandable explanations why the suggested alternatives are not viable will be immediately at hand.

Prior inconsistent statements provide one of the most common and frequently utilized tools of cross-examination. There is a panoply of potential sources of inconsistency. Prior articles or writings, prior testimony in trial or deposition in other matters, inconsistent statements in the current case, and other positions and statements of the expert that can be documented, such as by social media or other recordation, all are potential sources of impeachment efforts.

The seasoned expert, then, is acutely aware of the need to avoid placing contrary, outlying, or rash opinions in documentable form and makes adequate provision for tracking and recalling prior statements. Then there are no surprises.

Attempts at impeachment on the basis of prior inconsistent statements are best defeated by distinguishing the former statement as based on different facts and circumstances, by demonstrating how the prior statement has been taken out of context, or by offering a convincing explanation of the differing statement, such as ongoing research and development.

Dropping a new and inflammatory document on the witness is a favorite tactic. This circumstance often rattles the witness and promotes testifying errors. Demand should be made to see the document and time requested of the court to read and digest the document in advance of further questioning on it.

Some attorneys take great joy in attempting to show that the expert rushed to judgment. The context is usually the time of formation of the opinions in question. If it can be demonstrated that the opinions were reached early on, before development and consideration of full information, the suggestion can be made that the expert hurried the conclusions. There is also a possible inference that the expert is sticking with them as a matter of pride and to save face. If comprehensive information was acquired before the formation of opinions and if careful deliberation went into them, the subsequent discovery of additional information will not be likely to materially influence the opinions. This tactic is thus readily finessed.

Intemperate, overly rigid, or inflexible opinions, especially when stated in dramatic terms and couched in flowery or even inflammatory adjectives, give opportunity to paint the expert as more passionate than objective and as an exaggerator. Dispassion and objectivity should always be practiced both in written reports and in all testimony.

A related ploy is to select certain vocabulary or nomenclature used by the expert and request definitions. The idea is to catch the expert unprepared and create embarrassment and the impression of incompetence. The solution is advance preparation that will enable the expert to concisely and understandably define terms used.

Often experts include one or more disclaimers in their reports that limit or condition their conclusions. Disclaimers allow the opposing attorney opportunity to raise inferences that the expert is waffling. Disclaimers should have been used with care before the trial. It needs to be obvious to the jury from the testimony that they hear that the expert holds the stated opinions unequivocally and is committed to them.

Questioning Education and Expertise

Attorneys like to attack an expert's experience level and to point out any perceived lack of pertinent education and, if possible, the lack of university and postgraduate degrees.

By way of example, an architect who has a lifetime of working closely with plumbers, but who is not a plumber and has never worked directly in plumbing, may be asked by the referring attorney to comment on the work of a plumbing contractor. This is perfectly proper, and the architect is qualified to render opinions about the plumber's work. Nevertheless, opposing counsel may endeavor to make much of the fact that the architect expert has never personally laid pipe or worked with the tools. In the face of the lack of actual, hands-on experience, the expert should be prepared to offer testimony elucidating the intimacy of experience with the related field. Thus will be justified the legitimacy of the expert's commenting on the activities occurring in the related trade.

The profusion of advanced degrees, board certifications, and professional designations allows the suggestion that an expert otherwise well qualified is less so, absent one or more formal attainments. The mere absence of a certain degree or designation does not need to be fatal to an expert. The test before the jury is credibility. Frequently the expert with fewer formal degrees is actually the more persuasive. Experts need not be intimidated by questioning of their educational attainments. They then concentrate on giving intelligible, memorable, and convincing evidence.

The wisdom of an expert remaining strictly within the confines of verifiable and credible expertise is again emphasized. Opposing attorneys delight in inducing experts into testifying about matters that are beyond the boundaries of their supportable expertise. As has been repeatedly stated in this volume, this error is assiduously to be avoided.

Consistency and Inconsistency

An effective strategy used on cross-examination is to state a scientific principle involved in the case and to secure the expert's agreement with it. Next the expert is asked to agree to a recitation of the case facts. The follow-up, then, is to inquire whether the case facts are consistent or inconsistent with the scientific principle. Experts are often dramatically forced then, in front of the jury and to their detriment, to concede that the facts are not consistent. In similar vein, whenever it is possible for the opposition to present physical evidence that is inconsistent with the opinion, the validity of that opinion will be remarkably diminished.

Before undergoing cross-examination, experts should invest time and effort in verifying that their opinions are based on facts that are, in all respects, consistent with all the facts in the case, with accepted science, and that they will not be caught unawares by physical evidence that is inconsistent with their opinions.

Hypothetical Questions

Hypothetical questions are common on both direct and cross-examination. They need to be handled with care. Noted attorney Francis L. Wellman, author of a seminal book on cross-examination published in the early years of the last century, abhorred hypothetical questions. He said, "This is, perhaps, the most abominable form of evidence that was ever allowed to choke the mind of a juror or throttle his intelligence."[56] He goes on:

> A hypothetical question is supposed to be an accurate synopsis of the testimony that has already been sworn to by various witnesses who have preceded the appearance of the medical expert in the case. The doctor is then asked to assume the truth of every fact which counsel has included in his question, and to give the jury his opinions and conclusions as an expert from these supposed facts.[57]

The potential problem with hypothetical questions is that the jury may take the expert's answer to the hypothetical as evidence of the facts presented in the hypothetical. The jury needs to be made to understand that it is the truth of the question itself and not so much the answer that is critical.

If hypothetical questions are addressed to the witness by retaining counsel, they ideally will have been submitted to the witness well in advance of testimony. If not, the expert is vulnerable to challenge as having formed a precipitous opinion. The expert, further, should ensure that no facts are omitted from the hypothetical.

---

56 Francis L. Wellman, *The Art of Cross-Examination* (1932), 103.

57 Ibid.

Occasionally, moreover, experts will be asked on cross-examination to repeat the facts of the hypothetical. This is a timeworn but proven cross-examination technique. It exposes the danger and complexity of such questions, and, as hypothetical questions are usually long and involved, experts often experience difficulty in repeating them accurately and completely. The expert needs to be prepared to recite back the hypothetical facts without referring to notes. Otherwise, the opinion offered based on the hypothetical appears weak, and the potential for embarrassment of the expert is high.

As hypothetical questions often occur well before all evidence is in, another approach is for the examiner to add facts and then ask the expert to respond as to whether the additions would change the opinion. An expert should take care in adopting the premises of these essentially premature hypothetical questions.

Demonstrations, Calculations, and Tests

Asking experts, while on the witness stand, to make demonstrations, perform calculations, or do other tests may represent a successful line of attack against them. The failure to perform successfully and artfully can be devastating. Prior thought, planning, and, if necessary, practice in completing any sort of demonstration or calculations should be completed well in advance of trial.

Bad Questions and Bad Manners

It is often said that trial work is largely theater. Attorneys are fond of agitating, attempting to intimidate, and creating defensiveness and evasion in order to make an expert look bad to the jury audience. Derision, contempt, arrogance, moralizing, flagrant interrupting, and outright churlishness all are regularly used to distract and annoy the expert, with the hope that rising frustration will precipitate a loss of balance and temper and perhaps even induce the expert to respond in kind.

Attorneys are unusually sensitive to a witness's weaknesses, defensiveness, and evasion. If detected, they will be honed in on and effort will be made to exploit them. Defensiveness often leads to evasiveness, and both can give rise to the sense that the witness has something to hide. Any opinion offered should be offered confidently and decisively.

Efforts to annoy and ridicule are designed to elicit response in kind as well as lower the witness to the level of the attorney. However, in this eventuality it is the expert who suffers the more, as it is not the attorney whose testimony is before the jury for evaluation. As they do not testify, attorneys have much more latitude in terms of loutishness than do experts. Expert witnesses should not fall for this tactic. The old saw is true about not getting into a wrestling match with a pig: "You both get dirty, and the pig likes it."

Bad questions, as we have indicated above and at length, are to be expected. Unhappily, the attorney's preparation (or occasional lack thereof) notwithstanding, bad questions occur at trial as well. Compound, complex, and unintelligible questions are usually obvious to everyone in the courtroom. If the expert fails to understand a question, it is likely that the jury has done so as well. Within the boundaries of acceptable frequency, experts have leeway to ask that poor questions be rephrased.

Taking the Offensive and Turning the Tables

It has been said that the secret to successful humor and snappy repartee is the skill of careful listening. Experts are usually far better able to see the humor and get a good bon mot out of a conversation or situation when they practice very careful and precise listening skills. The same principle applies to experts who are successful at seizing the initiative in deposition or trial from a cross-examining attorney.

Good listening skills enable the expert witness to point out counsel's false premises and mischaracterizations. A ploy designed to make the witness look bad may in this way be converted to counsel being the one to lose out. Careful listening allows the expert to recognize and point out mistakes that the questioning attorney makes. It also reveals the "coolness under fire" of the expert witness and increases the very real possibility that attempts to induce the expert to become angry will fail and will visibly frustrate the questioner instead.

Experts should be aware of and seek opportunity to restate direct testimony. A request to explain in response to a complicated question can provide such an opportunity if counsel agrees. If counsel does not, the optics are reversed, and counsel looks bad. Also, asking to get off the stand and use a visual aid, chart, or model affords the potential of going back to and repeating and emphasizing compelling direct evidence.

Developing careful active listening habits enables an expert to consistently phrase answers in meaningful and memorable terms. An expert who listens well has much better potential of offering the keen turn of phrase that will stick in the collective memory of the jury, benefit the client's case, and enhance the expert's performance.

Having the Opposing Expert Present

Some attorneys consider it to be a good tactic (expense notwithstanding) to have their own expert present in the courtroom, sitting at counsel table, during the examination of the other side's expert. The purpose is psychological and is designed to pressure the testifying expert to be more conservative and neutral in rendering opinions before the jury.

Sundry Observations

Lastly, in keeping with the theme of full preparedness, attorneys earn detailed reputations and tend to try their cases consistently within the parameters of those reputations. Experts can research their opposing attorneys with relative ease. Habits, preferences, favorite tactics and antics, as well as general courtroom behavior, are all readily available to the careful researcher. The referring attorney and associates are the initial resource closest at hand.

Exceptional attorneys take great care in preparing their expert witnesses for trial, up to and including arranging for mock direct and cross-examinations by skilled questioners. Individual mentoring is also readily available. Experts who are serious about doing well at trial should seek these services with alacrity.

Trial is both adversarial and theatrical. These characteristics are nowhere more acutely demonstrated than in the cross-examination of expert witnesses. Cross-examination pits the intelligence, creativity, and even craftiness of the attorney against the learning, persuasiveness, and demeanor of the expert. Some experts may feel insecure at the thought of subjecting themselves to the "tender mercies" of attorneys in this arena. This does not need to be the case.

Fully qualified experts have all the education and experience necessary to survive cross-examination. Their intelligence and wit usually match that of the questioning attorney. Understanding the context, purposes, and tactics of cross-examination, as have been set forth in this chapter, will promote, if not guarantee, a capable and convincing response to the process. As experts amalgamate growing experience and familiarity with the process, they will likely not only gain great confidence but also derive a certain level of enjoyment out of the various challenges that cross-examination presents.

Our ancient system of justice is designed to seek and find the truth. Over the long run of history, it has succeeded magnificently well. It has built-in mechanisms for preventing abuse. But, in the end, little inoculates the expert from attorney contentiousness better than practice and preparedness. Whether by starting a referral with a creditable investigation and a well-crafted and complete report, by giving a polished and professional deposition, or by offering compelling trial testimony, the accomplished expert is always insulated by professional ability, experience, and quality work.

So, good preparation and a thorough understanding of the processes and practices of cross-examination complete the circle of competent expert participation in litigation. They also guarantee a winning performance at trial. Nonetheless, some additional pitfalls and impediments are seen to frustrate expert witness success and additionally to dampen the interest of some experts to make the commitment of getting into professional expert witness work. We will address these potential pitfalls in the next chapter.

CHAPTER SEVENTEEN

AVOIDING COMMON PITFALLS

We have been at great pains in this book to ensure that no one going into expert witness practice is under any illusion whatsoever that it is a professional bed of roses. As has been detailed more than once, the law is confrontational and adversarial: likewise, expert witness practice. This adversarial nature is inherent, historical, and fundamental to our manner of operating. All aspiring expert witnesses must be disposed fully to embrace it. The best is advice is blunt. Do not undertake this work unless you are sincerely ready for the rough and tumble of it.

The adversarial nature is such a marked operational distinctive of the law that if removed, the system would lose its character and effectiveness altogether. All who work in the system need to understand and accept that contention is an integral, expected, and necessary element of the process. Practitioners who are adversarial, litigious, and contentious are merely doing their jobs in the expected and time-honored manner.

The common pitfalls that experts will likely encounter when engaging in expert witness practice can usually be traced to an insufficient understanding of the adversarial nature of this business.

Most professionals, especially medical doctors, enjoy immediate authority with their patients and feel instant credibility from the moment they walk into the office. In direct practice it is assumed that architects, engineers, accountants, and doctors have nothing but the best interests of their clients or patients in mind, and that there is no purpose of higher priority than seeing them served and sent contentedly on their way. Professionals are accustomed to being sought out for their advice and having it be immediately accepted, believed, and acted upon. There is usually no underlying tension or suspicion between the professional and client, and the resolution of the client's problem is not based on any adversarial process.

For these reasons, one of the traps most easily fallen into by experts who undertake legal work is to fail to appreciate the pervasiveness of the adversarial character of legal practice and to operate under the basic assumption of authority and credibility that they daily enjoy in their nonlegal practices.

The professional expert does not enjoy automatic and unquestioned acceptance as an expert witness. Many experts are offended when this not accorded to them and consequently present as arrogant and aloof.

Jurors are the ultimate arbiters of the expert's work in a case. Experts are often surprised or nonplussed when they discover that jurors can have something of a split personality. Jurors who when physically ill, or who have a landslide problem in their backyard, or who need the designing of an addition to their residence, or who get an income tax audit and who seek and immediately accept the advice and counsel of their doctor, geotechnical engineer, architect, or CPA are the same jurors who suddenly become intensely skeptical of those very same professionals once empanelled and sitting in the jury box.

It is an odd irony that whereas jury duty is an activity that most people will go to great lengths to avoid, once selected, members of the public embrace the process with ultimate seriousness and dedication. In stark contrast to their usual experience, experts confronted by attorneys, judges, and, most importantly, jurors, need to earn acceptance and credibility just as any other witness. A high, and with some individuals, unaccustomed, degree of credibility is required to be sought and won by experts who venture into this field.

The incisiveness of jurors and their ability to acutely evaluate and accurately dissect the testimony of trial witnesses must not be underestimated. A fine and delicate touch is needful. Proceeding from a position of openness and self-effacement garners far greater favor than insistence upon what experts might be used to by way of automatic reliance and acceptance from their regular and usual customers.

Another pitfall arising from lack of awareness of the adversarial nature of the law can occur when a group of experts of the same field, say structural engineering or epidemiology, are retained by parties with conflicting interests in a case. There is temptation for them to get together among themselves and endeavor to work out a consensus solution to the case.

Once a matter gets to law, the legal process will resolve it, and the individual expert's participation on behalf of one of the litigating parties is confined, within the limits of all honesty and integrity, to advancing that client's interests and not collaborating on, say, an engineering or medical resolution to the case.

Then there is the matter of an expert's relationship with referring attorneys and entities. If coziness is a difficulty when it occurs with the other experts, it can be disastrous if revealed with referring attorneys or insurance representatives. Like everybody else, attorneys develop preferences and their own stables of favorite people. However, since law practice is in so many respects adversarial, opposing parties will be quick to expose and attack ongoing, collegial, congenial, and convivial professional relationships (normally the essential stuff of good business) between individual attorneys and insurance companies and their preferred, reliable experts.

Despite the fact that the expert will get to know well and often to like the referring attorney, maintaining a strictly professional, arm's-length relationship is needful. Failure to do so can lead to charges of lack of objectivity (and even claims, in first party matters, of conspiracy to harm the interests of policyholders).

Optics are of critical importance. If there is any justification for it at all, the expert will be asked how many golf outings or martinis the referring attorney has treated them to in the last year (as has been previously mentioned). Personal relations between the expert and the referring attorney are subject to discovery and subpoena, and they should be managed with great care. Strict neutrality and documentable, verifiable arm's-length relationships must be maintained between expert practitioners and those who retain their services. All appearance of undue influence, impropriety, working "hand in glove," and any manner of collaboration is to be assiduously avoided.

It is well to reiterate here that all contact with the referring attorney is discoverable once the expert is formally designated. For this reason, all conversations (including any preliminary or informal chats), discussions, emails, voicemails, notes, and letters (not only of the expert personally, but of support staff and possibly business associates) are subject to production and scrutiny. Regardless of how it starts, any referral could result in formal designation and should be handled accordingly from the inception.

In short, the best antidote to adversity is to stay independent and unaligned.

Yogi Berra's celebrated aphorism that "It ain't over till it's over" makes sense in both the competitive nature of baseball and life in general. If you keep on fighting, who knows? You might win after all. It is no surprise that the adversarial nature of the law works in just this way, and woe betide the expert who forgets Berra's comment and dials back intensity before the game is over.

Throughout nearly forty years of practicing law, I developed what I call a corollary to Murphy's law: "You haven't won till the money's in your bank account." From the perspective of claimant parties, there is very much that can go wrong in the process of converting a claim into money in the respective accounts of the client and lawyer. "Whatever can go wrong, will," and a claimant is well-advised to remember that litigation is a serious and competitive business in which there may be many a setback "twixt the slip (and fall) and the trip (to the bank)!"

Equally true is that Murphy's law works against referring attorneys and experts on the defense side. Attention to procedures and practices that will avoid these pitfalls is constantly needful, all the way through to the end of the process.

As has been alluded to previously, expert participation in a case is a threat to the monetary interests of the opposition. Every creative idea and legal maneuver will be employed to impugn the expert and to limit the scope of testimony or prevent it altogether. This is often done, as has also been mentioned, through a series of proceedings before the court called *in limine* motions, which occur just as the trial starts.

Through their *in limine* motions, the parties endeavor, among other efforts, to restrict or eliminate the participation in the case of the other side's expert(s). The grounds for potential success are limited only by the imagination of the parties and their attorneys. Some common ones are improper formal designation of the expert, late discovered conflict of interest, insufficient expert qualifications, failure to produce all required records and files, and failure to have commented in deposition on matters intended to be offered at trial.

The adversarial nature of law practice accentuates the ever-present danger that all the effort and expense of the expert's participation can be lost as the result of successful pretrial motions. Attention to detail, dedication to the task at hand, and unflagging vigilance to the very end of the assignment are essential to guarantee ultimate success.

Experts are occasionally tempted to curry notoriety and a level of distinctiveness by advancing novel positions or inventive theories. This sets them apart and fans interest. Often these views are outliers and occasionally even qualify as junk science. These sorts of temptations are to be avoided.

Previous mention has been made of how an asbestos manufacturer in the late 1970s retained a charming and well-spoken expert from a foreign country. He had a very pleasant accent and was a good talker. His big theory was that smoking tobacco was actually healthy for asbestosis sufferers. This gentleman's good appearance, complete with a sparkling audiovisual presentation including autopsy slides "supporting" his theory, never overcame the inherent lack of believability of his position. While he had all the gifts and talents to be a superior expert witness, his frankly outlying scientific position completely outweighed them. He discredited himself, and in the end did his client no useful good, all in spite of his considerable native abilities and charm.

An expert who desires to expand into this aspect of practice must willingly embrace the adversarial nature of the law, generally, and of expert witness practice, in particular. There is a tendency in modern society to view contention and partisanship as unhealthy and to prefer compromise and consensus. For obvious practical reasons that have been borne out by over a thousand years of experience, the law has by no means yet come under the influence of that movement.

Beyond the disquiet occasioned to many people by the confrontational character of expert work, there are other impediments that deserve brief mention.

CHAPTER EIGHTEEN

IMPEDIMENTA:
ADDRESSING SOME ROADBLOCKS TO
UNDERTAKING EXPERT WITNESS PRACTICE

No field of endeavor is without a certain amount of baggage and other detritus that retards the smooth and effective progress of its practitioners. So it is with being an expert witness. Why do some experts hesitate to engage in professional witness activities? Is there a level of fear of becoming involved with the law and with attorneys in particular? Is starting out in an entire new aspect of one's practice just too radical and scary?

Fear of (or perhaps more delicately stated, hesitancy about) attorneys is both rational and irrational. They can be intensely disagreeable, and experts need to enter the attorney world with their eyes open. More importantly, however, it is well to remember that, like any other large group of people, the bar is not monolithic. There are as many (if not more) who are genteel, respectful, and respectable as there are the brittle curmudgeons. Experts occasionally are reticent in the face of the battlefield that the law often is. However, they should consider that both the problem and its solution arise out of its partisan character. Whereas the competitive nature of the law practice might be said to promote contentiousness, that very system (which has two sides presenting their best cases to a neutral decision maker) limits, directs, and confines the contention to legitimate, productive, and useful ends.

The expert is free to pick and chose which attorneys to work with. Among the criteria for choosing may be both the attorney's affability as collaborator with the expert as well as the attorney's capacity for leavening and reducing the effects on the expert of a notably ferocious opposition. Of course, the stories that circulate are the most egregious ones. As has been pointed out in the context of potential disputes over the allowable scope of discovery, the vast majority of procedures are completed without any incident. Even then, only a small number of procedures experience issues. Most of those are amicably resolved, and it is only a tiny percentage that undergoes true conflict.

To close this section, some practical concerns are worthy of mention. Many experts hesitate to get into legal work out of concern that they may be taken away from their normal clients and work schedules. There is an understanding that expert work will have significant time demands and that these may be disruptive of schedules and work habits. These concerns are real and must be accepted by all who embark on this practice.

There will be time constraints and demands. There will be time crunches, crises, and emergencies. Medical doctors will be asked to schedule depositions and trial testimony and will be expected to appear, surgical obligations and the need to complete hospital rounds notwithstanding. The answer is in full acceptance of these considerations as an unavoidable component of this practice. The expert who is unwilling or unable to accept them should forego this kind of work.

Another worry is that additional administrative or overhead provisions will be necessary in order successfully to engage in this work. This concern is to a certain extent valid, but experience demonstrates that the percentage of overhead required to operate an efficient expert practice is usually less than that needed to operate a practice that services patients and clients directly.

In addition, there are agencies that supply these services; fee-based, high-quality, well-managed firms afford experts the full panoply of administrative services. These services extend from securing assignments, to providing examination facilities, to vetting and processing reports, to handling all billing. One of the attractions to expert work is that all administration can be left to these kinds of companies, with no impact on the individual's underlying practice.

There can be insecurity in becoming involved with unfamiliar people and patients and concern that attorneys will demand testimony that the expert is uncomfortable with. Resistance to the blandishments of attorneys who suggest the character or even substance of testimony is the hallmark of a quality expert. The ability to do so is wisely perfected early. As has been argued at length in this work, the expert's reputation for neutrality and objectivity is non-negotiable, and the preservation of it is "job one" for anyone desiring to get into consulting.

The new horizons offered by starting an expert practice need to be of sufficient interest to overcome any inertia created by attachment to the comfortable and familiar. The opportunities for professional advancement and monetary remuneration make the effort well worth it in the minds of most participants.

Every activity has its impedimenta. Those littering the pathway of the aspiring expert witness are no more or less significant than in any other professional activity. Likewise, there are two additional concerns that working as an expert shares with all commerce: getting picked and getting paid. No one stays in business long without succeeding at both.

CHAPTER NINETEEN

HOW TO ENSURE GETTING PICKED

Beyond all considerations of professional preparedness, good attitude, energy for the work, and overall diligent character, the prospective expert consultant faces the intensely practical challenge of becoming known and getting hired.

In real time, where-the-rubber-meets-the-road terms, word of mouth recommendation is doubtless the primary method for advancing an expert's reputation and for securing additional business. Person to person testimonial is the consistently effective tool for practice expansion. Word of mouth recommendation is extremely important and exceedingly common. The buzz of positive experiences that attorneys, their offices, and insurance claims representatives have had with a particular expert spreads rapidly. An attorney's experience of observing a superior expert in action for the opposition very often results in that attorney forming the strong resolve to retain such an excellent expert on the next case.

Little by way of formal advertising is observed in the current day and its absence is probably proof that such effort and investment would not likely be successful. Some experts put together marketing presentations that they shop around to prospective clients. These enjoy some success.

Over the years of my experience, the three most frequently mentioned attributes of experts that are cited in recommendation conversations are that the expert writes a good report, knows how to give a good deposition, and is easy to work with. The roundtable process detailed in chapter 7 is illustrative of this point.

A frequent occurrence at these roundtable events is discussion of whether an expert is needed for a certain case and, if so, who should be selected. Suggestions will be taken from individuals who have had experience with one expert or another. The virtue most often offered in favor is that the proffered expert "writes a great report." (Superior report writing is covered in chapter 9.) No other factor is remotely close in frequency of mention in these kinds of discussions. The identical experience is appreciated in calling colleagues for expert recommendations. Rarely will an attorney recommend an expert to a colleague without also commenting spontaneously that the individual writes a good report. (Giving good depositions and being easy to work with come in a rather distant second and third.)

Initial discussion is then followed with consideration of several additional factors.

Of immediate importance are specialty and experience, most notably with respect to medical experts. Neurosurgeons, neurologists, orthopedic surgeons, plastic surgeons, psychiatrists, and neuropsychologists are the most sought after medical specialties.

Current participation in practice in the subject profession is essential. Active, ongoing work doing audits, creating architectural plans and details, acting as general contractor, or plying one of the building trades is a sine qua non of expert selection. This, again, is most acutely significant in medical fields, particularly those specialties that frequently involve surgery, such as orthopedics, neurosurgery, internal medicine, plastic surgery, hand and foot specialties, and the like.

As has been discussed above, many surgeons, who have retired or for health or other reasons have discontinued their surgical practices, bristle at the insistence that an expert be in active surgical practice. They make the valid point that surgeons who are no longer practicing are able to fully evaluate patients within their specialties and, in fact, having abandoned active surgical practice, have more time and energy to devote to effective and meaningful consulting. The fact remains, nonetheless, that the current market for medical specialties involving surgeries emphatically requires (irrational though it may be) that experts be in active surgical practice.

Certifications and designations are extremely helpful. Many professions offer specialized certificates and designations attesting to study, knowledge, and experience in various subspecialties. Medical board certifications are a classic example. These are highly prized and greatly sought after by those who retain medical consultants.

Experience testifying both in deposition and at trial is very valuable. Skill in testifying may be learned from reading and study, but there is little substitute for the crucible of having actually faced cross-examination by a skillful attorney under circumstances when it truly counts. Experts who lack actual experience testifying should get it at the earliest practicable moment. Workshops, individual mentoring, and practice role-playing are helpful preparatory activities. In these ways, experts can develop a reputation for effectiveness, persuasiveness, ability to teach, and affability in front of the jury and then can promulgate this reputation among prospective clients.

Strict objectivity and fairness are non-negotiable. Experts and examiners are expected to be neutral and unbiased. They should consider themselves free to report findings and conclusions without concern for hewing toward or away from conservatism, liberality, extending the benefit of the doubt, sticking to the middle of the road, or any other philosophical orientation not otherwise held in good conscience by the examiner.

Expert witness practice is a service business. Once an assignment is accepted, the referring party and attorney are the customer: just as are private patients and clients. The legal side is prepared to invest heavily in expert participation in cases. In return, it needs and deserves consistent, willing, and cheerful effort.

Perhaps the greatest challenge in growing an expert consulting practice is overcoming the inertia of referring parties, who tend to gravitate toward already established individuals with whom they have had previous experience. Picking the old, tried, and true person, warts, wrinkles, and all, is the safe and easy move. Breaking through takes perseverance and a level of creativity on top of the several other attainments discussed both in this chapter and throughout the entirety of the book.

CHAPTER TWENTY

THE QUESTION OF FINANCE:
HOW TO ENSURE GETTING PAID

At the height of World War II, Winston Churchill wrote to President Franklin D. Roosevelt, asking him to expedite the conversion of American industrial output to war material production in order to assist the British war effort. At the end of his long letter, Churchill stated, "Last of all I come to the question of finance," whereupon he asked that his proposed arms purchases be extended on credit.

The question of finance is ever present and always important in all activities great and small. Expert witness practice is no exception.

Although the metaphor is much overused, financial arrangements between experts and their clients are the 800-pound gorilla in the room of civil litigation. We have spent significant time in this book discussing cross-examination techniques and lines of attack that can be expected from opposing counsel. Even the least experienced and most inartful attorneys will cover the financial angle on cross-examination. The subject will always come up.

After concerns about dealing with contention with opposing counsel, the concern most frequently raised by experts is the question of how to get paid. This is, of course, a matter of major practical concern. In addition, failure to effectively handle financial matters often utterly frustrates the high purpose of participating in, seeking, and doing justice that has energized many experts from the outset.

In some cases, the first step in ensuring that the expert is paid may be in deciding whether to take the case or to work with the particular attorney or not. It might be better from the outset, for example, to reject cases with little upside for winning significant money. Sources of payment, budgets, and financial viability of the referring attorney and office are legitimate inquiries and, if found wanting, justify passing on the case. Often a request for a sizeable retainer will weed out cases that are thinly funded.

Wherever possible, the practice of requiring cash on the barrelhead in advance should be followed. Doing so will often take grit and determination on the part of the expert. The effort and energy invested will be seen to have been worth it, however, as it is the best policy for avoiding money issues. In the end, it actually benefits all parties involved, including the expert receiving payment.

In any event, money matters must be clearly understood and agreed upon in advance. Payment obligations need to be strictly observed and complied with.

Assiduously to be avoided is the situation in which the expert's client falls behind in payment obligations, such that the expert goes into an important proceeding like a deposition or a trial with a significant balance owing. Allowing this sort of situation to develop opens potentially effective lines of attack on the expert's objectivity.

An expert owed significant money going in, it is implied, is forced to the position of making common cause with the client in order to secure payment. The expert thus loses credibility. This sort of impeachment then further promotes the potentiality that the expert will not be paid or will subsequently be compelled to settle for pennies on the dollar. The likelihood is then increased that the case will be lost or settled cheap. Experience teaches that when all has been lost or when disappointingly little has been gained, payment of a large expert bill is of virtually no priority at all to those who owe it.

From time to time, the question of finance is complicated in that sources of payment often are both the expert's own client as well as one or more of the opposing parties. In a personal injury case of moderate complexity, a physician may be hired on behalf of the defendant and will earn fees for the examination, medical records review, and report. Once the physician is designated as a retained expert, the plaintiff will have the right to request a deposition. Work in preparation for the deposition is payable by the retaining party, but the actual deposition time is paid by the plaintiff attorney.

One state's statutory provisions are quite comprehensive and generally typical. Under it, the noticing party must pay the expert's reasonable and customary hourly or daily fee. (Daily fees are allowed only if the expert is required to be available for a full day and necessarily had to forgo all other business.) (If expert fees are thought to be excessive, a party can seek relief from the court.) The designating party pays preparation and travel fees of the expert.[58] The expert, thus, has two sources of payment and two separate challenges for securing it.

In very complex cases such as construction defect matters, the several parties will usually each have their own expert. When expert discovery starts, the financial arrangements can become very complicated. In these cases, payment arrangements are usually agreed to in advance under the supervision of a court appointed special master and payment requirements formalized by the judge in a following court order.

In terms of the method of assessing charges, conceptually, experts might charge by the hour, by the case, or on contingency.

Contingency fee arrangements should be avoided. Many professional associations prohibit them. The American Academy of Orthopedic Surgeons requires that members "shall not agree to accept a fee that is contingent upon the outcome of the matter."[59] The vulnerability of contingency arrangements for insinuation of collusion and lack of objectivity is so obvious that it is difficult to appreciate how such arrangements could ever be justified.

---

58   California Code of Civil Procedure, Sections 2034.410-470.

59   American Association of Orthopedic Surgeons, Code of Ethics and Professionalism for Orthopedic Surgeons, Section V.C.

Charging a flat fee, that is, by the case without reference to the actual, specific time spent on the matter, is also a questionable practice. It is not desirable for the expert to receive a set or flat fee, even if it is paid in advance. This is because incentive to work the case as needed, as much as needed, with emphasis only on the areas needed, can be absent and the expert thus exposed to potential criticism.

As to the expert's own client, the clearly preferable approach is to work for agreed upon hourly fees payable for all work completed. This arrangement affords to the expert the freedom and flexibility to work the matter up and to devote time and energy in strict accordance with objective professional standards as well as the specific needs of the case. It also promotes the reputation of the expert for credibility and neutrality. Potential fodder for cross-examination is reduced. The expert is at liberty to forthrightly and boldly testify as to the hours worked, hours charged, and amounts per hour without excessive concern for impeachment over fees.

Per hour fees and the number of hours charged should, of course, be reasonable and customary within the expert's professional community. Many experts have differing per hour fees depending upon the complexity of the work involved. Hours for investigation and examination, research and record review, deposition, trial, and travel may have varying rates. This is a credible and acceptable practice that implies fairness.

Fees should be consistent. While lesser charges for travel or other routine activities are permissible, all clients, all courts, and all types of matters should be uniformly charged. Most experts have half day or full day charges for depositions and trial. This is legitimate as long as the expert can demonstrate that, in fact, an entire day (or half day) of other work was necessarily sacrificed for the proceeding. An expert's charges, once determined and promulgated, should then be consistently applied.

Charging discrepancies between clients, types of clients, and different insurance companies are to be strictly avoided.

Accounts need to be kept short. Statements should be submitted regularly and payment promptly secured. Account balances should not be allowed to build up. The expert is well advised to insist that the account be brought current prior to testifying in deposition or at trial. This avoids the expert having to give answers that imply interest in the outcome of the matter in order to be paid. Allowing balances to build makes the matter of getting current before any testimony the more complicated and difficult. The longer an expert allows account balances to build, the more leverage and incentive for payment is lost.

When requested by a nonreferring party to offer testimony, experts are entitled to be paid for their opinions. The only consistently workable alternative is cash-on-the-barrelhead, in advance. The requesting attorney should be asked to provide an estimate of the time that will be required for the deposition. Payment is required before the proceeding starts.

Some jurisdictions have special provisions for estimating expert time, such as the first hour payable in advance and time after that payable at the conclusion of the deposition. In any event, statutory constraints notwithstanding and bearing in mind the adversarial nature of legal practice, failure by the expert to secure advance payment is an invitation to significant collection effort at a minimum and occasional out-and-out nonpayment.

Sometimes an expert, such as a plaintiff's treating physician, is subpoenaed as a percipient witness only, and an attempt is made to limit payment to the statutory witness fee only. In those instances, only factual information may be elicited, such as dates and times of treatment and reading into the record of chart notes that are illegible. Experts should deny attorneys who use this strategy the benefit of any opinion testimony.

As alluded to above, in complex litigation with many parties, the court often issues a detailed pretrial order that covers several types of discovery matters including expert discovery and the payment of experts. These orders frequently appoint a special master or discovery referee to oversee the discovery process in general and the payment of experts for deposition.

These arrangements can be quite complicated, but they routinely provide at least some advance payment for the testifying experts and means of collecting fees in excess of the initial deposits.

Written contracts between the expert and the referring party are an issue. These are to be avoided. The burdens outweigh the benefits. The legalities of expert consultant work are straightforward, and there is probably not that much that needs formal memorializing by way of written contract. Any contract or memorandum of understanding is discoverable. Since the expert is often ultimately being paid by an insurance company, in most cases the making of a contract increases risk that under compulsion of discovery the document will become public. The further risk exists that the presence of insurance may come to the attention of the jury.

In money as well as many other administrative matters, association with a company that enlists experts, receives assignments from potential clients, and assigns them to its enrolled experts can be invaluable. These organizations typically handle all administrative details and defray all overhead expenses for a percentage of the expert fee. Some consider the percentage quite high. However, normal business overhead costs are commonly 55 percent or over, often much more in medical and dental practices, so that the percentage these companies charge is considered by most to be reasonable.

Such companies handle all aspects of marketing, securing assignments, assigning cases to specific experts, setting all details of examinations (some even provide examination facilities), providing transcription and deposition reports, and coordinating trial testimony details. Experts are thus freed to concentrate on the assignment, and their non-litigation practices are not burdened with the extra effort inevitably involved with forensic work.

Nothing overarches expert witness practice more than the question of money. Money and payment is surely a central element in all commerce, and litigation is no exception. Little has the potential for diminishing credibility and integrity more than the subject of remuneration.

Happily, all sides in a case will likely have experts, and both sides' experts will have payment arrangements. (Usually the respective experts' charges will be roughly equivalent so money issues should be offsetting.) Juries are acutely aware of the general costs of goods and services. They know that experts are highly paid. Experts' fees normally do not offend them if those fees are within reason and based upon rates customary in the community. Although routine, efforts to impeach experts on the basis of their charges are usually successfully controlled.

The question of finance is delicate and sensitive, but if thought out in advance and dealt with diligently and ethically, it is completely manageable.

CHAPTER TWENTY-ONE

ON RECORD KEEPING:
A CASE OF COMPETING AND
CONFLICTING CONSIDERATIONS

Significant controversy surrounds the matter of expert record keeping. Considerations include maintaining sufficient records both to enable full recall of previous activities in preparation of reports and for deposition or trial. Considerations also include keeping sufficient information for the purpose of accurate billing. In addition, considerations further include the essential element of developing a fail-safe method for tracking previous cases and assignments in order to avoid any hint of conflict of interest in undertaking new matters. Suitable software applications should be available for this purpose. Finally, experts need to have some access to the specifics of previous matters that they have worked on so as to avoid any potential inconsistent statements or positions.

Over against those considerations is the reality that after a surprisingly short amount of time the volume of records builds rapidly and storage and retrieval issues, including the costs thereof, will arise.

Even more importantly, all expert files are subject to subpoena by opposing counsel. This includes file jackets, labels, tabs, papers, documents, photographs, recordings (audio or video), emails, notes, calculations, billing statements and records, correspondence, and any drafts that have been maintained. In short, everything that the expert has in any file related to the matter must be produced and will be reviewed.

The reach of these kinds of subpoenas, furthermore, is not necessarily limited to only the case at hand. Thus the keeping of excessive material from past cases presents disadvantages in terms of providing potentially easy access to opposing counsel for impeachment as well as the aforementioned cost and administrative and logistical burdens of storage and indexing.

The solution is to strike the correct balance. Essential is maintaining enough information to refresh recollection when necessary, to corroborate that a complete investigation or examination was performed, and to justify any billings. On the other hand, experts need to avoid inclusion in the file and in the archives of all extraneous, unneeded, superfluous, or unnecessary items, documents, records, or information.

Some experts have the practice of filling their file with all manner of information and documentation, with the thought that in the event the file is subpoenaed, they will purge or "sanitize" it of any extraneous items. This practice is strictly to be avoided. For the expert's deposition, most attorneys will demand production of the file. Usually one of the first topics explored is whether the file presented is complete or whether anything has been removed from it. If items have been removed and if this line of inquiry is to be answered truthfully, suspicion will be raised as to the expert's credibility. It is a very difficult case to make that the items that were removed were somehow insignificant, duplicative, or "just preliminary notes and thoughts."

The far better practice is to assume from the moment of first contact that absolutely everything generated or received will form a part of the file and be subject to production. Experts should understand that in generating and gathering information in their files, they are creating evidence.

It bears repeating and as has been earlier suggested, it is wise to imagine that anything placed into the file could be blown up into a four-foot by eight-foot trial exhibit and placed by opposing counsel before the jury. Any item that would thus cause discomfort or embarrassment to the expert should be left out. This is a modified formulation of the so-called "Newspaper Test." Refrain from doing something (or in this context, putting it in the file) today, if it would be undesirable to see it tomorrow on the front page of the local newspaper.

Generally, the best policy for most fields of expertise is to include and to keep in the file the minimum of documentation and other material necessary to refresh recollection, to document that a professional and complete investigation or examination has been done, and to corroborate billing. Some experts (in construction defect cases, for example) have different considerations. In those types of matters, hundreds or even thousands of photographs may be taken to document site conditions, and these need to be retained, catalogued, and kept in orderly and accessible form.

Over a long and successful career, an expert will likely give a great deal of recorded testimony and may generate significant articles and other publications. In the modern Internet era, the expert's record is readily accessible. Striking the right balance between having access to previously stated positions and maintaining a volume of information which would be easily accessible to opposing counsel is a challenge.

This challenge is probably best addressed by carefully crafting opinions and taking care to ensure consistency at all times. Over the long run, it will be awkward, expensive, and time consuming to preserve copies of previous testimony. It is desirable to evolve a record keeping system that both ensures consistency of testimony over the years, but that at the same time requires the least practicable archiving of copies of prior testimony.

Although it is simplistic, some say, "Just tell the truth and you'll never have to worry." Certainly consistency is one key to lessening the need for record keeping.

Record subpoenas are directed either to individuals, their designated custodians of records, or to the custodians of records for nonindividual entities. Experts are not required to produce documents that either do not exist or are not in their possession and control. Recipients of record demands are not typically required to create documents or classes of documents that do not already exist. Thus there is incentive to limit the amount of records created.

Some experts designate another person, such as their office manager, administrator, or other logical person, as custodian of records. They place their records with that person for maintenance and preservation. In that situation, the expert can truthfully respond to requests to the effect that there are no records in possession and that another is the custodian of them.

It will not be long before the professional expert faces the question of disposition of files upon conclusion of the case. Many experts destroy files immediately upon learning that the case is settled. This policy has the virtue of minimizing record-keeping costs and reducing the amount of records available at any one time for subpoena. Other experts forward pertinent and essential parts of their files back to the referring attorney for safekeeping and preservation. This policy, while not destroying records, puts them out of the expert's possession and renders them more difficult to locate for subpoena.

Experts occasionally are asked to produce records indicating the proportion of cases handled respectively of claimant versus defense clients, or for particular attorneys, law offices, or insurance companies. It is not likely that the expert will categorize billing records in this way, and it is unwise to do so. In this connection, as with other record-keeping matters, the right balance should be found between maintaining sufficient current records to guarantee effective billing and collection while not exposing the expert and clients to undue invasions of sensitive financial information.

On balance, after a filed is closed, billed and paid and to the extent that records that are not needed for consistency in testimony and providing for ongoing and effective conflict checking, policies of earlier rather than later destruction are preferable.

In the matter of file making and record keeping, less is almost always more.

CHAPTER TWENTY-TWO

THE INTERNET, SOCIAL MEDIA, AND EXPERT WITNESS PRACTICE

Observers of developments in litigation during the past couple of decades will note the dramatic effect that the advent of the Internet and social media has had on the process. Countless litigants and witnesses have been surprised and embarrassed by the presentation before juries of the contents of their websites, blog posts, Facebook entries, or tweets, and the promulgation of videos showing them in a compromising or uncomplimentary light.

Most professional practitioners and experts have either individual or company websites. Ease of access is plainly the purpose of these sites. They are affirmatively for the purpose of exposing the expert's personal history, education, experience, and professional distinction. The expert's website should be reviewed for accuracy and completeness. Just as the CV needs to be in all respects fair and accurate, likewise the website. It is an irony of the Internet that just as it makes accessibility to the individual exponentially greater, it commensurately makes all website claims and data exponentially susceptible to quick and easy verification.

Blogging and tweeting have made the sharing of information, publication of thoughts and commentary, and generally giving vent to feelings and frustrations available to previously unimaginable numbers of writers and thinkers. Whereas the wideness of access may indeed be a positive development of the Internet age, it is true that the growth of access has often not been accompanied by quality vetting and editing.

There is a danger in blogging and tweeting of indulging temptation to make intemperate, impulsive, and poorly thought out posts. Search engines turn these up with minimal effort, and the potential for unflattering exposure of them against an expert at trial is high. Extreme judiciousness is needed in blog posting, writing letters to the editor, and otherwise documenting controversial, inflammatory, or unconventional matters.

Large numbers of personal injury litigants have been greatly compromised and have either lost their cases or had their recoveries severely reduced due to Facebook posts. In the minds of many, this is a narcissistic age. It is common to post one's adventures, accomplishments, attainments, and the like. This may be well and good, unless it is inconsistent with the poster's ongoing damages claim. One litigant in California recently claimed a serious shoulder injury with disabling residual effects. This litigant was quite persuasive but experienced a nasty shock when defense counsel played a YouTube video at trial showing him climbing El Capitan.

As electoral politics in the opening decades of the twenty-first century have powerfully demonstrated, the resurfacing of old videos containing unflattering statements is an ever-present danger. Virtually anything can be video recorded these days, with or without the subject's knowledge or consent.

In view of the profusion of surveillance cameras, cell phone cameras, and miniature video recorders, the average person needs to be acutely aware of the possibility that their activities are being recorded at any given time. Not only this, but also the trend of court decisions in recent years has been against the suppression of these kinds of recordings, privacy interests notwithstanding.

It is immensely simple to access anyone's electronic media information. Opposition research can economically and efficiently be outsourced to experts in digging up uncomplimentary information. Nothing is immune. Moreover, the use at trial of inconsistencies, gaffes, and excesses developed from electronic media almost always come as a surprise without advance warning. Beware the Internet!

CHAPTER TWENTY-THREE

THE CASE FOR EXPERT CERTIFICATION

Most professions have evolved means and methods for conferring upon their members certifications of one kind or another evidencing advanced qualifications, experience, and attainments. All manner of medical associations offer board certification in their varying specialties. State bar associations offer certifications in specialties such as criminal law, probate, family law, and workers' compensation. The Institutes offers the Chartered Property and Casualty Underwriter (CPCU) designation after completion of significant study and testing.

Suggestion is occasionally made at seminars, workshops, and professional meetings that a similar process should be considered in conjunction with expert witness practice. Thus, it is held, it would be possible to ensure that experts have received adequate training in the legal context and setting of their work. They would have been exposed to significant experience in effective report writing. They would have had practical and real experience in actual deposition and trial settings, wherein their skill and learning as experts would have been tested in actual practice. Finally, they would, as a result, be generally well inured to the realities of daily participation in this work.

Not all opinion is favorable. Many attorneys prefer that their expert witnesses, especially physicians, not be formally schooled in any matters involving litigation lest their neutrality and objectivity appear to juries to have been spoiled or their innocence and purity in the legal setting be compromised and undermined.

The contrarian position is at once understandable and hard to understand.

It is understandable in that there is clear need for experts to appear to be (and, in fact, to actually be) unaffected in the objectivity of their professional activities by their participation in the legal system. This cannot be denied and is of unexaggerated first importance. Nothing must ever be done that would in any way tarnish objectivity, neutrality, and fairness, as they are foundational pillars of the credibility that will always make or break an expert under the ever so incisive scrutiny of a jury.

It is hard to understand, however, in that continual difficulties are regularly encountered, year in and year out, case in and case out, with the unpreparedness, inexperience, ineffectiveness, and even uncooperativeness of experts.

On balance, the latter concerns argue more strongly for the view favoring greater formal preparation.

It is axiomatic, of course, that any such effort at developing a certification process would have at the outset to establish itself with the absolute guarantee of unbiased neutrality and fairness. It would from the start require the participation of all potential stakeholders. It would need to represent a truly bipartisan and "across-the-aisle" effort.

Assuming such a joint effort could be marshaled and carried forward, it is suggested that there should be at least three components of any certification program: formal education, practical training, and experience in practice.

Completion of course work in the following general areas of study, including passing an examination for each course, could be required:

- the law and the legal system

- objective and complete investigation

- effective communication, writing, and reporting

- depositions

- trial testimony

- record keeping and finance

Any curriculum would be specific, intentional, and strategic, comprising interactive elements, documented progress, results, practical experience, and testing.

Next, documented participation in specified numbers of separate cases that have required the writing of a formal report, the giving of a number of depositions in active cases, and the participation in a number of trials involving both direct testimony and cross-examination could be required, along the following lines:

- active and full participation, with report, in at least twenty-five litigated files

- completion of ten depositions

- direct and cross-examination testimony in at last five trials

Finally, a minimum of, say, five years in active and continuous professional expert witness practice could be required.

The obvious primary purpose of seeking and awarding an appropriate certification would be the elevation of the quality of expert witness practice. It is envisioned, moreover, that additional very practical results would be achieved, such as establishment of the expert among clients and potential clients as all the more qualified and suitable as the best choice for their cases. It would, in addition, offer the opportunity for experts thus certified to be remunerated accordingly.

Diligent effort would be advanced to secure the approval and support of various critical stakeholders, such as state bar associations and judicial councils, certification authorities of the various professions such as boards of medical qualifications, as well as accountancy, engineering, and architectural qualification authorities.

Only the passage of time will reveal whether the concept of establishing and perfecting a process for certifying experts as expert witnesses will, if attempted, gain favor and, if practicable, prove to prosper and, if successful, to endure. The proposal seems worth exploring in any event.

CHAPTER TWENTY-FOUR

AND LAST THINGS LAST:
CONCLUDING THOUGHTS

Hoping to stop the then growing trend to accept the participation of expert witnesses in law cases, Lord Campbell stated in the distant past, "Skilled witnesses come with such a bias on their minds to support the cause in which they are embarked, that hardly any weight should be given to their evidence." His efforts and those of many others to stop the movement favoring expert witnesses have, by the opening decades of the twenty-first century, manifestly failed.

The expert witness is now an indispensable element of legal practice. It is no longer a matter of discussion whether experts will participate in the law. The only question that remains is what will be the quality of that participation. It is hoped that the detailed discussions put forth in this book will prove to be helpful in materially elevating that quality.

In closing, it is suggested that the diligent and careful professional development that has been proposed here will in practice lead to significantly increased clarity of thinking and communicating, reporting, and testifying by experts. Exceptional clarity of mind and action will then lead to much greater competence in overall performance. Then, carefully developed and practiced competence will result in justifiable, measured, and communicable confidence by the expert. Of all attributes, steady, seasoned, and practiced confidence is the most fervently to be desired and is of greatest effectiveness across the entirety of expert practice.

Around 750 BC, the Old Testament prophet Micah was inspired to pose this question: What does God require of people other than to do justice, kindness, and humility? From the beginning, experts have participated in legal matters for the express purpose and goal of promoting and doing justice. Attainment of the goal of doing justice is not as elusive at it may at times seem, and the participation of experts greatly contributes to achieving it.

The advancement of justice will always be directly proportional to the increase of expert skill and ability.

ABOUT THE AUTHOR

Douglas L. Field attended the Universities of Madrid (Spain) and California (Berkeley), graduating from the latter in 1970. He then completed law school at King Hall (U. C. Davis) in 1973 and immediately entered the practice of civil litigation in Oakland, California.

After working as an associate and later partner at a large Oakland civil defense law firm, in 1980 he formed Taylor & Field, which engaged in all aspects of civil practice for both plaintiffs and defendants, including acting as panel counsel for several large insurance companies.

In 1997, Farmers Insurance Exchange recruited him, where he practiced civil defense litigation, including personal injury defense and construction defect. In 2003, he opened Farmers' staff counsel office in Stockton, California, and in 2006, he became the managing attorney of the Sacramento Branch Legal Office. There he oversaw fifteen to seventeen attorneys, averaging nearly 1,150 cases throughout each year. He retired from Farmers at the end of 2011.

During the entirety of his active practice, he has worked closely with expert witnesses in several fields including medicine, architecture, accounting, engineering, biomechanics, and accident reconstruction.

He has tried numerous jury cases to verdict.

After retiring from Farmers, he has dedicated his energies to the presentation of seminars and workshops for expert witnesses, primarily physicians, on various topics. He regularly sits as judge pro tempore in the Alameda County Superior Court and is a member of the Consuelo M. Callahan Inn of Court in Stockton, California.

His hobbies include the building and displaying of model ships and maintenance of his Spanish language skills.

Field and his wife, Sandra, have two grown children and four grandchildren. He divides his time between Danville and Woodbridge, California.

LEGAL DISCLAIMER AND WARNING

This book is informational **ONLY**. Although the author is a licensed attorney, nothing contained in it is offered in the manner of giving legal advice. The book is written with the understanding that and purchasers specifically agree that the author is not rendering legal or other professional advice of any kind. If the reader desires or requires legal advice, the services of a competent attorney should be sought. No representation is made that this volume contains all information available on the subjects discussed. It does not. The text offers general information only. The author is not engaged in giving legal advice on any specific or general matter and shall have no legal liability or responsibility to any person or entity for loss or damage caused or alleged to have been caused, whether directly or indirectly, as a result of any material or information contained in the book. The law and statutes constantly change and it is not possible to predict what developments may occur after publication of this volume. Every state and jurisdiction is distinct. Great variability exists among expert professions and disciplines, among cases and situations in which experts are employed, among attorneys who retain and use the services of experts and among experts themselves. In the event of any doubt or if legal advice is required, please contact your attorney or retaining attorney.

INDEX

attorney's fees
    liability for assessment of, 49
    recoverability of, 39, 76
audiovisual aids, 140
awareness, 56

B

bad faith, 76
bad manners, 154–55
bad questions, 154–55
benefits delivery system, 42
Berra, Yogi, 162
Berry, Samuel H., 25
biomechanical experts, xix, 2, 20–21, 40, 63, 82, 117
Bismarck, Otto von, 41
blogging, 183–84
"But For" test, 34

C

CACI (California Civil Instructions), 35
cadence, 110, 144
calculations
    performance of, 154
    verification of, 114, 116
California
    conduct of medical examinations in, 51
    exchange of expert witness information in, 52–53
    and reports, 86
California Civil Instructions (CACI), 35
California Code of Civil Procedure (CCP), 44
California Discovery Act, 44
cameras, 184. See also photography, use of; video recorders; videotaping (of depositions)
Cardozo, Benjamin, 27
careless conduct, 32, 34

case evaluation
    accuracy as paramount, 61
    defined, 58
    examples, 62–64
case value, 58
cash-on-the-barrelhead, in advance, 176
causation
    as element of negligence case, 32, 34–36
    as subject on which experts are permitted/encouraged to opinine, 89
causation analysis, 89
cause
    alternative causes, 89, 150
    concurrent cause, 34–35
    identifiable cause, 36
    intervening cause, 36
    legal cause, 28, 34–36, 91
    proximate cause, 28, 34–36, 91
caution, 56
CCP (California Code of Civil Procedure), 44
cell phone cameras, 184
certifications, value of, 170
Chartered Property and Casualty Underwriter (CPCU), 185
charts, 127, 138, 140, 156
chronological sequence, 36
Churchill, Winston, 172
civil case, life/stages of, 12, 40
civil defense attorneys, 12
civil discovery acts, 44
civil judgments (against expert), 123
civil law countries, 27
claim, conversion of to money, 94
claims continuum, 66–69
clichés, 89
codes, 26
coefficient of friction testing, 84
cogency, 99
collaboration, 2, 17
Colorado, and FRCP, 44
Common Law
    adaptability and evolution of, 30–31

adversarial nature of, 28. *See also* law,
   as adversarial
  distinctions of, 27–28
  origin of, 26–28
communication. *See also* language;
  report writing
  breakdowns in, 2
  importance of, 29, 78
  improvement of, 3–4
  organization and skill in, 142–43
  realms of, 4
  written requirements of, 14
companies/agencies that supply experts,
  166–67, 177
complex answers, 109
concurrent cause, 34–35
confidence, 17, 28, 89, 98, 121, 123,
  134, 136, 144, 155, 157, 189
conflicts of interest, 77, 79–80, 163
connecting (with jury), 137–38
consistency, 10, 16–18, 85, 89, 99, 104,
  108, 122, 152–53, 156, 170, 181–82
constitutions, 26
construction defects, 20, 23, 40, 84,
  127, 174, 181
consultant, compared to designated
  expert witness, 53–54, 56–57
contention/contentiousness, 93–94,
  96–97, 157, 165
context, of expert witness activity, 2–3
contextual understanding, lack of, 1
contingency fee arrangements, 94, 123,
  174
contracts, written, 177
contributory fault, 60, 62–64
conversing (with jury), 137, 138–39
conveying (to jury), 137, 139–40
convincing (jury), 137, 141–42
convoluted answers, 109
cooperation, 2, 4–5, 18
court system, understanding of, 2
courts, written decisions of, 26
Covenant of Good Faith and Fair
  Dealing, 73–74
coziness, 76, 161

CPCU (Chartered Property and
  Casualty Underwriter), 185
credibility
  assumptions of, 160
  attorney's role is to question, 123
  attorney's techniques to reduce, 121
  as built slowly and deliberately, 99
  challenge of preserving to the end, xx
  construction of, 17
  damage to, 122
  as diminished by exaggeration, 109
  effect of grace and good cheer on, 129
  enhanced by active current practice
    in profession, 117–18
  essence of, 137
  of expert as granted automatically,
    xix, 23
  foundational pillars of, 186
  from giving attribution/recognizing
    sources, 141
  guessing equals loss of, 108
  as hallmark of expert testimony, 99
  impact on of removing items from
    file, 180
  loss of, 173
  as matter for jury to decide, 23
  as needing to be earned, 160
  of professionals with patients/clients,
    11–12, 92, 159
  remuneration as potential for
    diminishing of, 177
  as secured by well-written report, 86
  as test before jury, 152
criminal history (of expert), 123
criticism of other experts, 119
cross-examination
  described, 120, 157
  intention of, 134
  questions during, 147
  secret to successful, 146
current active participation in practice,
  117–18, 169–70
Curriculum Vitae, 100–101, 121–22,
  183
custodian of records, 182

D

damages
  additional types of, 39–41
  categories of, 36
  as element of negligence case, 32,
    36–41
  for injury, 30
date-sensitive deadlines, 5
Daubert Trilogy, 21, 22
deductions, and case value, 60, 62
demand letter/brochure, 82
demand process, 83–85
demonstrations, 140, 154
depositions
  admonitions at beginning of, 109
  and advance agreements, 110
  advantages of, 48
  answering only questions asked, 108
  arguing with questioner, 109
  contrasted with trials, 132–33
  defined, 48, 106
  described, 48–49
  document dump, 128
  fee for, 55–56
  how lawyers prepare for, 111–13
  and humor, 109–10
  likelihood of, 82
  locations of, 126
  overall perspective of, 107
  precision of language during, 109
  predictable attack lines and cross-
    examination techniques, 120–31
  preparation for, 114–15
  primary purpose of, 133
  principles of good deposition
    testimony, 114–19
  as realm of communication/
    communication event, 4
  as stage of civil case, 12
  taking time during, 110
  travel to, 55
  and truth-telling, 107–8
  and volunteering/guessing, 108
  waiver of reading/signing transcript,
    110

designations, value of, 170
destructive testing, 84
dictation, as compared to direct typing
  of reports, 87
differential diagnosis, 36
digital photography, use of, 83
direct examination, elements of, 134–45
direct language, 143
disclaimers, 151
discovery
  defined, 43
  as liberal, 45, 46
  scope of, 45–47
  as stage of civil case, 12, 40
  typical vehicles of, 44
discovery statutes, 47
discretionary rulings, 95
dispassion, 90, 96, 105, 118, 136, 151.
  See also passion
disputes, 46–47, 94, 96, 166
disruption, 95–97
distinctiveness, 163
document demands, 49–50, 82
document dump (at deposition), 128
documentation, study of, 114–16
documents, dropping new and
  inflammatory document on witness,
  150
drama, 133, 146
due process, 43–44
duty of care, 31–33

E

earnings, loss of, 38
editorial we, 90
85/14/1 Rule, 94
electronic media information, 184
emotional distress, damages for, 76
empirical evidence, reliance on, 28
enhancements, and case value, 60–61
equivocal words, 144
equivocation, 89
euphemisms, 143
evasions, 149

of experts, 20, 56, 107, 117
 physician/patient privilege, 46
probability, 35, 36, 130
professional discipline (of expert), 123
professional witness attacks, view of
 juries about, 149
professional witness (term), 19
pronouns, use of, 144
property defects, 33
protections, and experts, 56
proximate cause, 28, 34–36, 91
psychometric testing, 116, 117
psychromatic chart, 127
punitive damages, 36, 39, 42, 59, 76
pure exposure value (PEV), 59, 60

Q

QUACKERY (acronym), 100
quarreling, 94
questions
 about education and expertise,
  151–52
 answering only those asked, 108
 bad questions, 154–55
 for cross-examination, 147
 difficult and tricky, 129–30
 as eliciting examples, 135
 gotcha-type, 90
 hypothetical, 19–20, 130, 153–54
 lousy questions, 121
 preparation for of expert with
  counsel, 135–36
 at trial, 133–34

R

rambling, 109
ranges, use of, 90
recency, principle of, 143
record keeping, 179–83
recordings, 94–95
reduction for fault, 60
referral process, 13

regulatory law, 26
reliance on others, 114, 117
reluctant symbiosis, 7, 8–9
report writing
 additional attributes of good reports,
  89–92
 guidelines, 87
 importance of, 85–86, 169
 outline, 88
 as realm of communication/
  communication event, 4
requests for admissions, 49
research, 114, 116
rhythms, of lawyers, 110
roadblocks, 165–67
rocket docket, 11
Roman law, 27
Roosevelt, Franklin D., 172
rote report formats, 91
roundtable discussions, 64–65, 169
rushes, 14

S

sanctions, 47, 95, 96
scheduling changes, 14
scientific field of inquiry, experts as
 learned in, 2–3
scientific knowledge, 22
scientific method, 22, 36
self-effacement, 161
settlements
 discovery as liberal to promote early,
  45, 57
 percentage of compared to trials, 12,
  57, 68
 unreasonable failure to settle within
  policy limits, 77–78
shared liability, 35
sheepishness, 149
shortcuts, 115
single and combined limits (of
 insurance policies), 71
site inspections, 83, 84, 88
site views, 83, 94

CPSIA information can be obtained at www.ICGtesting.com
Printed in the USA
LVOW11s2123101014

408314LV00001B/39/P